Corey J. L. Walker, Erik D. Bair, Siobhan Schneider & Joanie L. Grife

Iowa Workers' Compensation An Insider's Guide to Work Injuries

7 <u>Deadly Mistakes</u> To Avoid If You Are Hurt At Work

and

Injured Iowans First Fee Schedule™
(Why our Injured Iowans First Fee Schedule™
may be right for you)

Iowa Workers' Compensation Attorneys
**Corey J. L. Walker, Erik D. Bair,
Siobhan Schneider & Joanie L. Grife**
Walker, Billingsley & Bair

<u>Ankeny</u> 2605 SW White Birch, Ste. 110- 515-964-5664
<u>Des Moines</u>- 2545 E. Euclid, Ste. 120- 515-440-2852
<u>Marshalltown</u>- 25 North Center St.- 641-352-4747
<u>Newton</u>- 208 N. 2nd Ave. West- 641-792-3595

www.IowaWorkInjury.com

Printed in the United States of America.

ISBN: 978-1-59872-776-0
LCCN: 2007923165
$19.95

InstantPublisher.com
PO Box 985
Collierville, TN 38027
www.InstantPublisher.com

INDEX

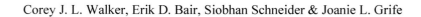

Page left blank intentionally.

If you or a loved one have recently been injured at work, you are probably confused or worried about what steps to take next:

▸ Will I be paid for the time I'm losing from work?

▸ Is the weekly amount that I am being paid correct?

▸ Will my future medical bills to treat my injuries be paid?

▸ What if I don't make a full recovery and cannot return to my former work?

▸ What will the insurance company offer me for my work injury?

▸ How will I know if the insurance company's settlement offer is fair for my injuries?

▸ How can I find an attorney to represent me who specializes in work injury cases?

▸ How can I avoid hiring an attorney who is not experienced in work injury cases?

If you or someone you care about has any of these concerns, then please keep reading this book.

"DISCOVER WHAT INSURANCE COMPANIES DON'T WANT YOU TO KNOW ABOUT YOUR WORK INJURY CLAIM!"

We Are Not Allowed to Give Legal Advice In this Book!

We know the arguments the insurance company will make —and so should you—even before you file your claim. When you were injured you began a climb up a mountain to regain your respect and financial freedom. The insurance industry spends hundreds of millions of dollars each year hiring doctors to fight against you and other injured workers. We will be in this fight together. However, we are not allowed to give you legal advice in this book. We will offer you suggestions and identify potential mistakes, but please do not construe anything in this book as legal advice because it is not.

(**WARNING:** THIS BOOK CONTAINS GENERAL STATEMENTS AND IS NOT INTENDED AS LEGAL ADVICE OR LEGAL OPINIONS. THIS BOOK DOES NOT CREATE AN ATTORNEY-CLIENT RELATIONSHIP. DO NOT ACT OR RELY UPON THE INFORMATION IN THIS BOOK WITHOUT SEEKING THE ADVICE OF AN ATTORNEY BECAUSE CHANGES IN THE LAW OCCUR FREQUENTLY, AND YOU SHOULD CONSULT WITH AN ATTORNEY WITH RESPECT TO YOUR PARTICULAR CASE.)

Note: If you are already represented by an attorney, this book may raise questions for you. We have had many clients hire us after firing their attorney who did not return phone calls, did not explain the process, were not experienced in handling injury cases, etc. You can still use this book to increase your knowledge, but we won't take your case if you are currently represented by an attorney!

Who Wrote This Book

- and -

"Why Should I Listen?"

First of all, we want to thank you for requesting this book. We have written this book so that injured workers have the inside information they need before hiring an attorney or dealing with the insurance company in the battle for just compensation. As we will discuss later in this book, you do not need to hire an attorney in every case. However, you should have the inside information contained in this book before an insurance adjustor pressures you to settle or you make a costly mistake.

At age 14, Corey (pictured on the left) began working for his grandfather in the concrete construction business during the summer school break. The work was hard, hot, and long, but provided him with framework for his character. His grandfather always told him to get a good education so he did not have to do hard labor for the rest of his life.

Corey graduated from Newton High School in 1990 and played on the 1988 state 4A runner-up football team. After he graduated from high school, his mother purchased an appliance store and he began working on weekends and during the summer delivering refrigerators, washers, dryers and other heavy equipment. He would also help his grandfather when he needed extra help on job sites. He attended Central College in Pella where he graduated in 1994 and then went on to Drake Law School. After his first year of law school in 1995, he began working at Walker & Billingsley (now known as Walker, Billingsley & Bair).

Siobhan (pronounced sha-von pictured to the right of Corey) grew up in a suburb of Chicago in a family where work ethic was valued above nearly everything else. Her father was up before dawn and would come home from work each evening, just as her mother left for her job, and asked Siobhan and her siblings "What have you done to justify your existence today?" The question was not rhetorical, her dad wanted an answer, and they had to give him one. At 14, she began working part time at a local stable, mucking out stalls, and feeding the horses. From there, she held a number of part time jobs throughout high school and college, including driving a forklift at a home improvement store. She has learned to value the building blocks of any good employee: show up, work hard, and give as much effort to working for others as you would want for yourself. Siobhan strives to remember the teachings of her parents, and provide her clients with the high-quality professional, personalized attention that she would expect from her own attorney.

Erik grew-up on the east side of Des Moines and graduated from East High School in 1993 followed by Iowa State in 1998. While in high school he worked at Hy-Vee and during college he was a laborer with the City of Des Moines in the summer and worked at Mary Greeley Hospital during the school year. He attended Drake Law School where he graduated in 2001.

Joanie is an Iowa transplant as she was born and raised in Virginia where she grew up on the family farm. She worked side by side with her parents growing apples and peaches and raising cows. She was always active in athletics and received a scholarship to attend Bluefield College in Bluefield, Virginia where she played volleyball and softball during her career. Also, she worked very hard in the classroom completing her Bachelor of Science in Criminal Justice with minors in Psychology and Sociology in only 3 years. She met her husband Rich who grew up in Montezuma while she was attending Bluefield College.

After graduating from Bluefield College in 1997, she moved to Sioux City where her husband played baseball for the Sioux City Explorers. She took a job working as a paralegal, but had her dreams set on law school. In 2000, she started law school at the University of South Dakota and continued to work as a paralegal. She had originally planned to move back to the east coast, but fell in love with Iowa. After graduating from law school in 2003, she found a job in Marshalltown. Her husband also found work as the baseball coach at Marshalltown Community College. They have lived in the Marshalltown area since 2003 including living in Haverhill where she served on the city council and as mayor.

Corey, Siobhan, Erik and Joanie have experienced firsthand what it is to put in a hard day of work. They have also seen the lives of co-workers changed by work injuries. Their years of hard work allow them to better understand their clients, many of whom have been injured working physically demanding jobs. They are here to give a helping hand to injured workers and help them get back on their feet after a work injury.

Together, they have been representing individuals against insurance companies and big corporations for almost 50 years. They practice primarily in workers' compensation and injury law so more than 95% of their practice involves work injuries, accidents and personal injury cases. With hard work and personal attention they are committed to **Leveling the Field** Between **Injured Iowans** and Insurance Companies.^{TM}

- o <u>Experience</u>- Represented More than 1,200 Iowans Injured in Work Injuries, Car Accidents, and Other Personal Injury Accidents
- o <u>Active Trial Practice</u>- More Than 400 Trials Handling Many Workers' Compensation Cases Throughout the Appeals Process
- o Corey has an <u>www.Avvo.com</u> Attorney Rating of "Superb"- 10 out of 10
- o Corey has been Featured by the USA Today, Des Moines Register, Chicago Tribune, KCCI TV, WOI TV, ABC News Radio, etc. and been Named "Top 100 Trial Lawyer" by The National Trial Lawyers

---

- o Members of the Iowa and American Associations for Justice- Corey has been a Board of Governor with IAJ since 2001
- o Active in Drafting and Lobbying for Legislation to Help Injured Iowans
- o Corey was raised in Newton, graduated from Central College and Drake Law School, has been married to his wife Beth since 1998 and they have 2 children (son and daughter)
- o Siobhan grew up in a suburb of Chicago in a working class family who instilled a hard work ethic in her. She attended Tulane University in New Orleans and graduated from Drake Law School in 2007. She has been married to her husband Mike since 2004 and they have two daughters.
- o Erik was born and raised in Des Moines, graduated from East High School, Iowa State and Drake Law School, has been married to his wife Jessica who is a nurse since 2003 and they have two daughters
- o Joanie was born in Virginia, but fell in love with Iowa where she has lived since 2000. Her and her husband Rich have 3 children (an older daughter and twins, a boy and a girl)

Our law firm has 7 attorneys and represents individuals throughout Iowa in workers' compensation, car accident and other personal injury matters. To better serve our clients we have offices located in Ankeny, Des Moines, Marshalltown and Newton along with by appointment only locations throughout Iowa.

We realize that your work injury may be the most important event going on in your life right now. Your case will be personally handled by one of our attorneys – not a paralegal. We have represented hundreds of Iowans hurt at work and have also represented many families of deceased loved ones killed at work. While each case is different, and past results cannot be used to predict future success, we can tell you that we have been privileged to help our clients and their families recover millions of dollars in settlements and verdicts for their work injuries.

Corey has been featured in news reports by the following:

Corey has been recognized by the following organizations:

Why Did We Write This Free Book?

(Insurance Companies and Lawyers!)

We have heard too many **horror stories** about **insurance companies** taking advantage of people before they have a chance to talk to an attorney. For years one major insurance company encouraged Injured Iowans to not hire an attorney and tried to settle their case early on. Once a case is settled with the insurance company either in writing or on the phone, most likely you will be bound by the terms of the agreement. We wrote this book so that Iowans injured at work have the inside information they need before hiring an attorney or dealing with the insurance company in the battle for just compensation. As we will discuss later in this book, you do not need to hire an attorney in every case. However, you should have the inside information and know the insurance company's tactics which are contained in this book before an insurance adjustor pressures you to settle.

We also wrote this book because our rules of ethics encourage us to educate the public. The preamble to Rule 32 provides:

> As a public citizen, a lawyer should seek improvement of the law, access to the legal system, the administration of justice, and the quality of service rendered by the legal profession. As a member of a learned profession, a lawyer should cultivate knowledge of the law beyond its use for clients, employ that knowledge in reform of the law, and work to strengthen legal education. In addition, a lawyer should further the public's understanding of and confidence in the rule of law and the justice system because legal institutions in a constitutional democracy depend on popular participation and support to maintain their authority.

13

Frankly, this method of talking to you also saves us time. We have packed a ton of information into this book, and it saves us the hours of time that it would take each day just to talk to all of the new potential clients who call. We cannot and will not accept every case and each year we turn down many cases that simply do not meet our case selection criteria. So, rather than cut you short on the phone, writing this book gives us a chance to tell you what you need to know so that you can make an informed decision about what steps to take with your case. Even if we do not accept your case, we would like you to be educated about the process so that you don't become an insurance company victim.

Most attorneys require you to make an appointment in which you would get some of the information that we have provided here. We believe that you should be able to have this information right now, and without any pressure. The hiring of an attorney to represent you is a very important step that should not be taken lightly.

We are also sick and tired of lawyers with a reputation for handling hundreds of cases at a time who have no intention of taking your case to trial, and this book should help you to identify those lawyers before you hire one.

Fewer Cases— Which Allows Us to Spend More Time For <u>You</u>

We are not your average Iowa law firm. We are "different." We have the legal know how combined with personal service and attention to details to **Level the Field** Between **Injured Iowans** and Insurance Companies.^{TM}

We don't rely on a high volume of cases. We don't claim to handle every type of law under the sun. We don't want to, and we do not need to.

Each year, we accept a limited number of work injury, personal injury and accident cases from the hundreds of people who ask us to represent them. We are not a "mill" law firm and our paralegals and assistants do not negotiate our cases with the insurance company. Fewer cases means more time for you and, we believe, better results overall.

Together, for almost 50 years we have represented injured workers throughout the state of Iowa and beyond. Most of the cases are referred to us by former clients and by other attorneys. If we accept your case and you are not local to us, we will come to you.

Communication- We take pride in having a personal relationship with our clients and communication is a key part of this. Rest assured that we will explain the legal process to you, answer all of your questions and keep you informed about your case including sending you copies of letters. Also, unless our time is being devoted to a trial, we will return your phone calls and respond to your emails within 24 hours during the workweek.

Sometimes the best advice you can get when you are thinking about a workers' compensation petition for arbitration (which is similar to filing a lawsuit in a civil case) is that you do not have a claim that can be won. If that is true, we will tell you. We'll also tell you when we think you are better off handling a claim yourself—without an attorney. But, if your case passes our test and we accept it, you can be assured that you will receive our personal attention. We will aggressively represent you, keep you up to date on what is happening in your case, and give you our advice as to whether you should settle your case or whether we should go to trial.

We will fully explain all fees and costs to you before we start working on your case. Together, as a team, we will decide on the best tactics for your case.

Dedicated to <u>Leveling the Field</u> Between Injured Iowans and Insurance Companies^{TM} by Fighting for <u>Justice</u> and Respect^{TM}

Fewer Cases - More Time For <u>You</u>

7 MYTHS ABOUT IOWA WORK INJURIES- WORKERS' COMPENSATION CASES

➢ The insurance adjustor is there to help you with your work injury case.

➢ If you are reasonable with the insurance company, then they will be reasonable with you.

➢ If you have a medical case manager assigned to your case you have to let them in the examination room during your exam.

➢ All attorneys who advertise that they handle workers' compensation cases have the same skills, education, tools and experience to handle your case.

➢ All attorneys charge the same fees in work injury cases.

➢ All attorneys are personally involved in the cases they handle.

➢ The workers' compensation system is so simple and easy to understand that injured workers should represent themselves.

What is a Workers' Compensation Case?

Let's start at the very beginning: Just what is a workers' compensation case? Attorneys say that they do "work injuries" or "workers' compensation cases" and yet what does this mean? A workers' compensation case is any type of claim where a person has been injured or killed while on the job. The legal requirement is that the work injury arose out of and in the course of employment. There are 3 basic types of workers' compensation benefits available:

1. Medical Benefits- Lifetime medical benefits for medical treatment, including doctors' appointments, prescriptions and mileage expenses related to your work injury.

2. Healing Period/Temporary Disability (TTD/TPD) Benefits- These are the weekly payments made to an injured worker while they are healing from their work injury and are not able to return to their job, are only able to work a limited number of hours or are not making as much as they were before the work injury.

3. Permanent Benefits- At some point the doctors will say that you have healed as much as possible which is also known as maximum medical improvement (MMI). At that point, your benefits change from temporary to permanent. If your medical condition heals and you are left with no permanent problems, then you probably do not have a claim for permanent disability benefits. If you have a permanent impairment rating and/or permanent restrictions, then you are likely owed permanent disability benefits. You need an attorney who understands the specialized workers' compensation laws.

What Must be Proven to Win a Work Injury Case?

The law does not require that a person is compensated for every work injury. You must prove that you were on the job working when you were injured. However, please keep in mind that there are special exceptions like falling in the employer's parking lot which are also considered a work injury, horseplay which is not considered a work injury, etc.

What if I Previously Sustained an Injury and I am Injured Again? Aggravations

Under Iowa Law, you need only prove that a work injury caused a material and substantial aggravation of a preexisting condition for it to be considered a work injury. That means just because you have had a prior injury to the same body part, you may still be entitled to benefits.

Also, if you previously sustained a scheduled member injury (arm, leg, etc.), whether or not it was work related, and then you sustain another scheduled member injury then you may be entitled to additional benefits under the Iowa Second Injury Fund. If you qualify for 2nd Injury Fund benefits then the extent of your permanent disability benefits will be based upon the factors used when determining industrial disability just like a back, shoulder, neck or brain injury.

What if I Was Hurt in Iowa, but my Employer is From Another State?

Generally, the Iowa Workers' compensation system has jurisdiction over all injuries which occur within the state of Iowa subject to a few exceptions. Iowa Code § 85.3 and 85.72.

What if I Was Hurt Outside The State of Iowa?

Depending on the language of your employment contract, where you were hired, time spent in Iowa or other factors, you may still have an Iowa Workers' compensation claim. For example, it is common for Iowa trucking companies to put language in their contracts stating that if you are hurt at work, you agree that you will have an Iowa Workers' compensation claim. It is not necessarily a bad thing to have an Iowa case because compared to other states, Iowa has some of the best benefits available.

Can I Sue My Employer For Pain and Suffering?

No, generally you are not allowed to sue your employer for pain and suffering. When the Iowa Workers' Compensation statute was passed in 1913, there was a trade-off made between employers and employees. While an employee does not have to prove fault or negligence like they would in a car accident case for instance, the trade-off is that the employee is not allowed to recover pain and suffering damages. Under what is known as the "exclusive remedy doctrine", an employee generally only has a workers' compensation claim against his or her employer for work injuries. There are exceptions to this rule such as what is known as "gross negligence" and you should consult an attorney to find-out if your case meets one of the exceptions.

What if I Work for the U.S. Government or U.S. Postal Service?

Then you do not have an Iowa Workers' Compensation case, but rather a claim under FECA- Federal Employees Compensation Act. We do not handle FECA cases, but you can go to www.FecaAttorney.com for more information including an attorney who does practice FECA law.

What is an FCE- Functional Capacity Evaluation or Examination?

A Functional Capacity Evaluation (called FCE for short) is testing done by a physical therapist. It usually involves a series of physical tests performed at the request of the physical therapist. The process can take from a few hours to more than 6 hours over 2 days. The length of the FCE will depend upon who the physical therapist is and what type of FCE they will be performing. There are several different FCE systems which are designed to determine what you should and should not do given your physical issues.

What Does MMI Mean and Why are They Ordering a FCE?

A FCE is usually ordered once you have reached maximum medical improvement referred to as MMI. Once you are at MMI, in the opinion of the doctor you are treating with, you are as good as you are going to get. Do not let this discourage you because there are many doctors with many different opinions. You are always allowed to seek medical care and treatment on your own, but usually it will be at your own expense, unless you are successful in obtaining alternative medical care described elsewhere in this book. Also, keep in mind that you have the right to a 2nd opinion once their doctor says you are at MMI and has evaluated you for a permanent impairment rating. Your right to a 2nd opinion is discussed in more detail elsewhere in this book.

What Can I Expect at the FCE?

First of all, please keep in mind that under Iowa law you are not required to attend a FCE examination, but failing to attend one can have a significant impact on your case. If you are not comfortable with proceeding with a FCE you should contact a qualified work injury attorney to discuss the specifics in your case so you can decide what is best for you. Also, there are many very important things you should know about what to do and not to do during the evaluation. Here are some of the tips we provide to our clients when attending a FCE:

1. Giving Your Best, "Full Effort"- You should try hard and give a full and honest effort in the tests without injuring yourself. There are a number of tests built into the evaluation that will determine if you are giving full effort. Therefore, even if the therapist tests an area of your body that was not injured, you still need to give full effort. One of the keys to the FCE test is that as long as someone comes in and gives their very best effort during the test, then it should result in a valid test.

2. Restrictions- if you are currently under restrictions given by one or more doctors I would recommend that you bring your written restrictions with you to the FCE and show the therapist these prior to the evaluation.

3. Medications- I would recommend that you do not take your pain medications in the morning on the day of the examination, unless you know that your employer will allow you to take the pain medications while working.

4. The therapist is not your friend and you need to be careful about what you say. It is <u>not the time</u> to make "wise-cracks"; say negative things about the insurance company, your employer, the defense attorney, your doctors or anyone else for that matter; or exaggerate your symptoms. For example, if you tell the therapist that you can only sit for 5 minutes at a time, then you better be standing up every 5 minutes or they will record this as being inconsistent with what you said. The therapist will write down in his/her report what you tell them so be honest and stay with the facts.

5. You need to make sure that you fully understand the therapist's instructions as to when you should stop an activity before performing the test. For example, if the therapist tells you to continue the exercise until the pain increases to the point where it is uncomfortable, ask the therapist to define that for you. Does it mean that you would be uncomfortable doing it every day at work or that it causes you increased pain? Make sure that you understand when the therapist wants you to stop.

A FCE is a very important part of your workers' compensation case and can significantly impact if you are able to go back to your job, how much compensation you receive, etc. The above represents just some of the tips we provide to our clients along with a detailed consultation so they are fully prepared and know what to expect at the FCE.

Do You Really Need An Attorney To Settle Your Case?

You definitely <u>do not</u> need an attorney for every work injury case. For example, our office will only accept your case if your injuries are permanent. If your injuries are not permanent and your claim has been denied, then you may be owed some benefits, but handling smaller cases would take time away from the more significant cases that we handle. Iowans who have sustained serious work injuries are beginning to realize that the insurance company for their employer is not there to help them and that they should consider having someone on their side.

What if the Your Employer Does not Have Insurance?

If at the time of your injury your employer does not have insurance and is not a registered self-insured employer then you have the option of either filing a workers' compensation case or filing a civil suit for damages. However, please keep in mind that obtaining a judgment against your employer is only half the battle because you have to collect upon the judgment. While Iowa law requires that every employer must have workers' compensation coverage or be an approved self-insurer, a significant number of employers ignore the law, and injured workers pay the price.

What Are the Benefits of Hiring an Attorney?

- You will have someone on your side fighting for you, protecting your rights and explaining how the legal system works.

- Relieve your stress of dealing with the insurance company. Also, our experience in dealing with insurance companies will help ensure that you receive the full value of your case.

- Take away the pressure of collection agencies and medical providers calling about your medical bills as they will be directed to contact us.

- Someone who can give you an idea about what your case is worth

- Trial Experience. If your case is not able to be settled you will have a trial attorney working hard to achieve the best possible result.

When Should You Hire an Attorney?

· Serious Injuries- If you have sustained serious personal injuries requiring surgery or other significant medical treatment. Before you make a potential mistake in your case you should have a qualified attorney on your side to help you through the process. (Hint: There are many issues involving unemployment law. For example, if you are fired and have been hurt at work there is a right and wrong time to apply for unemployment benefits. You need an attorney that can also help you through the unemployment process because it can have a significant impact upon your work injury claim). The earlier you hire a qualified attorney to help you, the less likely that you will make a mistake that could cost you thousands of dollars. Keep in mind that if you are currently receiving weekly benefits, the attorney you hire should **not** take any percentage of your current benefits and most will not require you to pay a retainer or any up-front fees.

· Permanent Injury- If it did not appear that your injuries were serious at first, but after you are done with treatment you receive a permanent impairment rating and/or permanent restrictions or if you still have ongoing pain or limitations then you should talk to a qualified work injury attorney to find out if you should receive industrial disability or Second Injury Fund benefits.

· Denied claim- If your work injury claim has been denied by the insurance company or your employer then you will need an attorney if you want to pursue the matter further.

How Do I Find a Qualified Work Injury Attorney?

Choosing an attorney to represent you is a very important task, but can be quite confusing given the numerous choices. Your decision should not be made on the basis of advertising alone. The Yellow Pages are filled with attorney advertisements that all basically say the same thing. You should not hire an attorney solely based upon their Yellow Page ad or a commercial that they run. You should not even hire us until you are convinced that we are the right attorneys for your case.

How Do You Choose a Qualified Work Injury Attorney?

How do you find out which attorney is the best for your case? We believe that there are certain questions you should ask that will lead you to the best attorney for your case no matter what type of claim that you have. It will involve you spending some time and reading some materials, but choosing the right attorney is an important decision. Workers' compensation cases are far too specialized for someone who does not regularly practice in these areas. Too often, we have looked at cases that inexperienced attorneys handled. The insurance companies keep track of and know which attorneys actually go to court and try cases and those who just settle. The insurance companies use this information to evaluate their risk. One of the first questions many insurance adjusters will ask when presented with a serious case is: Who represents the injured worker? **If this is important to the insurance company, should it not also be important to you?** If you are represented by an attorney who does not have extensive experience going to court and trying serious injury cases or who "handles" a lot of work injury cases but settles them all, then your case may be at risk.

So, How do You Find Out Who is Good in Your Area? Here Are Some Tips

1. Get a referral from an attorney that you know. He or she may know someone who specializes in the area of law that you need. If you don't know anyone at all, then you can use the Internet and Yellow Pages to find names and information.

2. However, **make sure to ask each attorney if they have information just like this book,** a DVD and/or a web site so that you can find out more about qualifications, experience, results and verdicts, what past clients have to say and how they plan to handle your case before you walk in the door.

3. The Yellow Pages can be a good source of names. However, you need to understand three things: First, not everyone advertises in the Yellow Pages. Many of our cases come from referrals from other attorneys and from satisfied clients. Second, be careful about the ads from a single attorney who touts too many different specialties (for example family law, criminal law, personal injury, workers' compensation), no one can do everything well. Third, be careful because this advertising typically attracts a lot of cases, including the small cases that we do not accept. Make sure that the attorney you hire is selective enough with his or her cases that your important case does not become just one more file in the pile.

4. The Iowa State Bar Association does have an attorney referral service. However, please understand that attorneys have signed up **and paid a fee** to be listed in certain specialties. Their names come up on a rotating basis. This is another good source for an initial appointment. Just take the questions we talk about here to that interview.

5. Be careful about any attorney who rushes you to sign a contingent fee agreement. A contingent fee is not the right fee for every type of personal injury case. We know of cases in which attorneys have taken large fees on cases in which they did very little to deserve the fee. In fact, some attorneys have lost their license to practice law for engaging in these practices. Also, beware of an attorney who immediately wants to send you to one of his or her doctors.

6. Ask your attorney if he or she is licensed in the state where your case will be filed. We believe that an attorney who is not licensed in the state where the case will be filed is at a disadvantage when it comes to negotiating with the insurance company. The insurance companies know who is not licensed and thus cannot actually try the case. We recently came across a tragic story involving an out-of-state attorney who evaluated an Iowa car accident case. This attorney kept the file for almost two years and gave it back to the client just one week prior to the expiration of the statute of limitations. The problem was that the attorney told the client that he had another year to file the case, but this was based on the statute of limitations in his own state. The client was then prohibited from pursuing his case in Iowa.

7. Here are factors and good points to look for and question your attorney about. Note that not every attorney will meet all of these criteria, but the significant absence of the following should be a big question mark.

> • **Client Satisfaction-** Ask the attorney to show you what their past clients have to say about their legal services.

• **Experience actually trying cases** — ask the attorney how many cases they have actually tried before the Iowa Workers' Compensation Commissioner. What is their track record? Have they achieved any significant results, verdicts or settlements? Does the attorney have a list of verdicts and settlements available that you can look at? Don't accept the "All my cases are confidential" line! The greater number of cases actually tried with substantial verdicts and settlements achieved, the more likely the insurance companies will respect the attorney. Past results are not a guarantee of the future, but past results do demonstrate some level of experience and success. Also, what do their past clients have to say?

• **Respect in the legal community-** does the attorney teach other attorneys in Continuing Legal Education courses?

• **Membership and role in Justice Associations-** in your area, you can certainly find lawyers who are members of the Iowa Association for Justice and the American Association for Justice, formerly known as the Association of Trial Lawyers of America (ATLA). All of these organizations provide extensive education and networking for trial lawyers. Also, being actively involved, such as being on the board of an association shows the attorney's dedication to helping Injured Iowans.

• **Publications-** has the attorney written anything that has been accepted for publication? This is another sign of respect that the legal community has for his or her skills and experience.

31

• **Attorney Rating-** Does the attorney have a rating of "superb" on the attorney rating site www.Avvo.com? This rating involves a combination of what the attorney has written; education; experience; what other attorneys and clients have said about the attorney; and various other factors.

Once You Have Decided on an Attorney, Make Sure You Both Understand Your Goals and You Understand How the Relationship Will Work

1. How will your attorney keep you informed about the progress of the case? In our practice, we usually send a copy of every letter and pleading in the case to the client. We also take time to explain the "pace" of the case and in what time frames the client can expect activity to take place. Our clients are invited to call or email us at anytime. If we are not available, then we will usually call or email you within 24 hours, unless our time is being devoted to a trial. Also, our assistants can schedule a "telephone appointment." Finally, you are invited to make an appointment to come in at a time that is convenient to you.

2. Find out who will actually be working on your case. Make sure that you and your attorney understand who your case will be assigned to. There are a lot of things that go on in a case that do not require an experienced trial attorney's attention. On the other hand, if you are hiring an attorney because of his or her trial skills, make sure that that person is going to be trying your case for you.

If you decide that we are not the firm for you, we recommend that you contact one or more of the following attorneys listed in alphabetical order:

Harry Dahl- (515) 224-1070

Tom Drew- (515) 323-5640

Erik Luthens- (515) 222-1697

Martin Ozga- (515) 226-2117

R. Saffin Parrish-Sams- (515) 222-3133

Mark Soldat- (515) 222-3133

TIME MAY BE RUNNING OUT!!!

The law imposes rigid time deadlines in which to provide notice and file a petition in your case. These *time limitations* can be as short as **90 days** from the date of the incident to provide notice to your employer. The failure to act timely to protect yourself can completely eliminate your right to recover!

Notice of Injury- Under Iowa Law the injured worker has only 90 days from when he/she knew or should have known that they sustained a work related injury to provide notice to their employer.

Time to File Claim- Generally, the employee only has 2 years from the date of injury to file a petition with the Iowa Workers' Compensation Commission. However, if the employee has been paid workers' compensation weekly benefits then the time may be extended up to 3 years from the date of the last payment. However, we always recommend that an attorney review your case well within the 2 year time frame because the risk is too great to take a chance. For example, sometimes an employee has actually not received workers' compensation benefits, but rather has been paid wages, short-term disability or other benefits that do not qualify for the 3 year extension. Note: the payment of medical expenses alone does not qualify.

(WARNING: THESE ARE GENERAL STATEMENTS AND NOT INTENDED AS LEGAL ADVICE. THERE ARE MANY EXCEPTIONS AND YOU SHOULD CONSULT AN ATTORNEY CONCERNING YOUR PARTICULAR CLAIM AND THE APPLICABLE STATUTE OF LIMITATIONS AND ANY AVAILABLE EXCEPTIONS SUCH AS IF THE INJURED PERSON IS A MINOR. ALSO, THE FILING OF A CLAIM OR SUIT SOLELY TO COERCE A SETTLEMENT OR TO HARASS ANOTHER COULD BE ILLEGAL AND COULD RENDER THE PERSON SO FILING LIABLE FOR MALICIOUS PROSECUTION OR ABUSE OF PROCESS).

THE INJURED WORKERS' BILL OF RIGHTS

Iowa Law has recognized the needs of its injured workers since 1913. The law requires every employer to obtain workers' compensation insurance (or for the employer to register with the State of Iowa as being self-insured) to cover their workers. Even the best employer, however, is not likely to tell you all you need to know. If you are injured in a work accident or suffer from an occupational disease caused by your work, then Iowa law says that you have the following rights:

(**WARNING:** THESE ARE GENERAL STATEMENTS AND NOT INTENDED AS LEGAL ADVICE. CHANGES IN THE LAW OCCUR FREQUENTLY. YOU SHOULD CONSULT WITH AN ATTORNEY CONCERNING YOUR PARTICULAR CASE.)

1. Lifelong Medical Care: Your employer and/or their insurance company are responsible for paying for all medical care necessary to treat your work related injury. This includes all forms of care and treatment, whether hospital, medical, therapy, nursing, diagnostic testing, surgery, physical rehabilitation or pain management. However, generally your employer and/or their insurance company get to choose your medical providers. The right to medical care and treatment may continue for the rest of your life for conditions related to your work injury or occupational disease.

2. Right to Medical Treatment: You always have the right to seek medical care from any medical provider that you choose. However, please keep in mind that your employer and/or their insurance carrier will generally only pay for medical care that they have authorized or approved.

Also, if you have health insurance they may reject the claim as being a work related condition.

3. Payment of Medical Care Including Mileage:

- **Medical Expenses:** Generally, your employer and/or their insurance company has to provide you with medical care and treatment. This includes them paying for all treatment that they offer to you. However, there are some circumstances when they can be held responsible for paying medical expenses that you incur with medical providers not approved by them. For example, if your work injury claim has been denied, they lose control over your medical treatment. If your injury is later determined to be work related, they would be responsible for the costs. There are other limited circumstances when you can seek medical care with a provider who is not approved and they will be required to pay for it.

- **Mileage Expenses:** You are entitled to be reimbursed at the following rates for all mileage you incur going to and from doctors' appointments, physical therapy visits, etc. for travel during the time periods listed:
    $.555 per mile- July 1, 2012 to June 30, 2013
    $.565 per mile- July 1, 2013 to June 30, 2014
    $.56 per mile- July 1, 2014 to June 30, 2015

(Note: the mileage amount usually changes every July 1)

4. Right to Refuse Medical Care: You have the right to refuse any medical procedures or care that you do not want. For example, if the company doctor recommends surgery you do not have to proceed with surgery. However, please keep in mind that not proceeding with surgery may have an impact upon your case.

5. Weekly Check While You Recover And Cannot Work: While you are healing and unable to work, you will receive weekly checks to replace your usual earnings. This applies both if you are completely unable to work (known as TTD- temporary total disability benefits) or if you return to work, but are working less than 40 hours per week (known as TPD- temporary partial disability benefits). The amount of your weekly payment is called your "rate" which is discussed below.

- **Rate:** The amount of your weekly payments, also known as your "weekly benefits", is based upon your average earnings prior to the work injury, known as your AWW- Average Weekly Wage. If you are paid on an hourly basis, generally your rate will be based upon your average wages for a 13 week period prior to your work injury, excluding short weeks (weeks in which you should have, but did not work a full 40 hours for a reason like illness, etc). Your weekly rate is based upon your marital status, your number of exemptions, and your AWW- Average Weekly Wage multiplied times 80% of your spendable weekly earnings. For a link to the chart where you can look up your rate based upon AWW, etc. go to www.IowaWorkInjuryRate.com. Note: there are different rules that apply if you were injured while working on a part-time job, were paid a salary, etc.

There is no minimum rate for TTD- Temporary Total Disability benefits or TPD-Temporary Partial Disability benefits. TTD benefits are paid at your weekly rate while TPD is calculated based upon the amount of your AWW- Average Weekly Wages minus what you are making while working either a different job for less money or less hours X 2/3. For example, if you were making $600 per week before you were injured and the doctor has released you to work 4 hours per day at your normal hourly rate of $15 per hour then you would be making $300 per week. $600 - $300 = $300 X 2/3 = $200 in TPD benefits in addition to the wages you make while working 4 hours per day.

PPD- There is both a minimum and a maximum average weekly wage for permanent disability benefits based upon the statewide average weekly wage. These amounts change each year and for work injuries which occurred from July 1, 2013 until June 30, 2014, the minimum- AWW- Average Weekly Wage is $270 and the maximum is $1,419. If your work injury occurred before or after this time frame you can find a link at http://www.iowaworkforce.org/wc/publications.htm.

Your rate is very important because it determines how much compensation you receive. For example, if you are owed 100 weeks of benefits and your rate is $252 then your total compensation is $25,200. However, if you are owed 100 weeks of benefits and your rate is $575 your total compensation is $57,500. Our experience is that in about **50% of our cases**, the employer/insurance company has **underpaid the employee** by using a lower weekly rate **than what is owed**. That is why in every case we verify that you have been paid the proper rate as it can make thousands of dollars of difference. Note: Permanent benefits are paid weekly, but some benefits may have accrued such that they owe you a lump-sum, plus interest.

Time Missed from Work to Attend Appointments- If you are required to miss work to attend doctors' appointments, physical therapy or other medical appointments then you are to be reimbursed for the time you miss from work. Iowa Code § 85.27(7) provides that when an employee attends medical appointments he/she "shall be paid an amount equivalent to the wages lost at the employee's regular rate of pay for the time the employee is required to leave work. For purposes of this subsection, "day of incapacity to work" means eight hours of accumulated absence from work due to incapacity to work or due to the receipt of services pursuant to this section. The employer shall make the payments under this subsection as wages to the employee after making such deductions from the amount as legally required or customarily made by the employer from wages. Payments made under this subsection shall be required to be reimbursed pursuant to any insurance policy covering workers' compensation."

6. Money for Permanent Disability: If your work injury or occupational disease causes a permanent disability, also known as a permanent impairment rating or functional impairment rating, then you are entitled to money for the resulting disability. The amount of the benefits is based upon the body part(s) involved, the nature and extent of your disability and the amount of your average weekly earnings prior to your work injury.

Examples of Unscheduled Member Injuries:

Shoulder- Percentage based upon 500 weeks of available benefits. For example an 8% body as a whole shoulder impairment rating generally equals a minimum of 40 weeks of benefits. However, depending on many factors, including lifting and activity restrictions imposed, lost wages, etc. an 8% shoulder impairment rating could result in 100 weeks or more in benefits.

Back- Percentage based upon 500 weeks of available benefits. For example a 10% body as a whole back impairment rating generally equals a minimum of 50 weeks of benefits. However, depending on many factors including lifting and activity restrictions imposed, lost wages, etc. a 10% back impairment rating could result in 120 weeks or more in benefits.

Neck- Percentage based upon 500 weeks of available benefits. For example a 15% body as a whole neck impairment rating generally equals a minimum of 75 weeks of benefits. However, depending on many factors including lifting and activity restrictions imposed, lost wages, etc. a 15% neck impairment rating could result in 150 weeks or more in benefits.

Brain and Mental Injuries- Percentage based upon 500 weeks of available benefits. Sometimes you will not receive an impairment rating for a brain injury or mental health injuries such as depression, anxiety or PTSD- post traumatic stress disorder. However, if you have a permanent brain or mental health condition which has impacted your ability to earn a living then you may be entitled to receive permanent disability benefits.

Burns to Skin and Nerve Injuries- CRPS/RSD (Chronic Regional Pain Syndrome)- Even if your work injury is to a scheduled member, if you have sustained a burn or been diagnosed with one of the above nerve injuries or another type of nerve injury then your case may be considered an injury to your body as a whole. Depending on many factors including your ability to work, lifting and activity restrictions imposed, lost wages, etc. you may be entitled to a percentage of 500 weeks of benefits.

Respiratory and Circulation Injuries- These injuries include occupational asthma and injuries to arms or other body parts when the circulation has been affected like in Reynaud's syndrome.

Examples of Scheduled Member Injuries:

Arm- 250 weeks, e.g. a 10% arm impairment rating equals 25 weeks of benefits.

Hand- 190 weeks, e.g. a 20% hand impairment rating equals 38 weeks of benefits.

Fingers- Thumb- 60 weeks, 1ˢᵗ Finger- 35 weeks, 2ⁿᵈ Finger- 30 weeks, 3ʳᵈ Finger- 25 weeks, 4ᵗʰ Finger- 20 weeks. For example, a 40% impairment rating to the 1ˢᵗ finger would equal 14 weeks of benefits. Please note that injuries to fingers may not count as an injury to a hand for 2ⁿᵈ injury fund or other purposes.

Leg- 220 weeks, e.g. a 15% leg impairment rating equals 33 weeks of benefits.

Foot- 150 weeks, e.g. a 30% foot impairment rating equals 45 weeks of benefits.

Toes- Great/big toe- 40 weeks
Any other toe- 15 weeks

Eye- 140 weeks

Loss of hearing in one ear- 50 weeks

<u>Loss of hearing in both ears</u>- 175 weeks

<u>Permanent disfigurement, face or head</u>- 150 weeks

NOTE: If you do not know which category your injury fits into please contact us. Also, you may be entitled to additional benefits for a scheduled member injury depending on whether or not you have sustained previous injuries, etc. For example, you may qualify for 2nd Injury Fund benefits.

- <u>2nd Injury Fund:</u> If you previously sustained a scheduled member injury (arm, hand, leg, knee, foot or eye) even if it was not work related, and then sustain a work related scheduled member injury you may be entitled to additional benefits under the Iowa Second Injury Fund Act. Please keep in mind that prior medical conditions such as arthritis, carpel tunnel, vision loss, etc. followed by a scheduled member work related injury may qualify you for additional benefits. If you think that you may qualify for the 2nd injury fund, please give us a call, and we can help you determine if you qualify.

- <u>Permanent Total Disability:</u> If you sustain an unscheduled member injury, injuries to both hands, arms or legs; or a qualifying 2nd Injury and are no longer able to do any work, then you may be entitled to receive permanent total disability benefits which pay you a weekly benefit for the rest of your life.

- <u>Death:</u> Damages for the death of a worker are available for the wife, husband, and/or dependent children of the deceased. This can include a spouse if there was a common law marriage. Also, sometimes people who were not related, but dependent upon the deceased may recover. Damages are compensation for the lifetime of the beneficiary.

- Retirement: It is seldom a good idea to retire while you have a workers' compensation claim pending. If you retire, then you are taking yourself out of the labor market and will not lose any earnings in the future because you are retired. A retirement can result in you receiving little or no permanent benefits.

- Additional Disability Benefits If Your Condition Worsens: You may be able to "review and re-open" your claim after an initial disability award if the injury worsens. The request to "review and re-open" your claim MUST BE MADE WITHIN THREE YEARS of the date on which you last received workers' compensation disability benefits. In order to make this request you must file a petition with the workers' compensation agency. Keep in mind, that the standards to "review and re-open" a case are high and it can be difficult to obtain any additional compensation.

7. **IME (Independent Medical Examination)**- Once the doctors have said that you will not make further improvement (called MMI- maximum medical improvement) and evaluated you for a permanent impairment rating, you have the right to a 2nd opinion and to be evaluated for a permanent impairment rating. Under Iowa Code § 85.39, once you have been rated the insurance company is required to pay for an examination with a doctor of your choice called an IME (independent medical examination). This is a very important right and the doctor you choose is critical. You do not want to just choose any local doctor to do your IME as some doctors are more likely to give an opinion to help the insurance company.

43

There are only a handful of qualified IME doctors around the State of Iowa. We can help you choose the best IME doctor for your case depending upon your injuries and where you live.

8. Right to Your Job- Under Iowa law your employer is not supposed to fire you for filing a workers' compensation claim. However, you can be terminated for other reasons such as absences, work problems, work restrictions, etc. Also, subject to some exceptions (for example if you are a union member) your employer does not have to find you work if you are unable to return to your old job because of permanent restrictions.

9. Right to Find Another Job- Leaving your job does not end your workers' compensation claim. Just because you may be receiving workers' compensation benefits, does not mean that you have to remain employed with the same employer. However, leaving your job while you are still being treated may impact your case and the compensation that you receive.

10. Right to Seek Alternative Medical Care- If the medical care offered by your employer and/or their insurance company is not reasonable then you may file a petition for alternative medical care. However, please keep in mind that there are specific legal requirements that must be completed before filing such a petition. Also, if the employer denies liability in your case then the petition will be dismissed. For more information, look for our section on Alternative Medical Care in this book.

THE WORST THING YOU CAN DO

IS WHAT TOO MANY PEOPLE DO – DELAY OR DO NOTHING!

These days, **doing nothing at all is one of the worst things you can do.** It's hard enough to make ends meet and getting injured should not have to make matters worse. Too many people have told me they wished they had acted sooner before important witnesses moved and could no longer be found, before delays or gaps in their medical treatment proved damaging to their case. We have encountered many people who have suffered serious injuries from work injuries who failed to seek the "right" legal advice. Some of these people haven't gone to an attorney because they did not know they had the right to compensation, some were intimidated and some had bad experiences with other attorneys in the past.

WHERE DO WE GO FROM HERE?

What Do We Do for You in a Workers' Compensation Case?

Here is a list of the tasks we most likely will do in your case. Please keep in mind that each case is different, and that not all of these tasks will be required in every case. They are:

- Initial interview with the client

- Educate client about work injury claims

- Gather documentary evidence including accident reports, medical records and bills

- Hire an investigator, if necessary, to interview witnesses, locate witnesses, etc.

- Talk to the client's physicians and obtain written reports as needed

- Collect other evidence such as videos of the work site and job descriptions

- Decide with the client whether an attempt will be made to negotiate the case with the insurance company or whether a petition should be filed

- If a petition is filed, prepare the client, witnesses and healthcare providers for depositions

- Prepare written questions and answers along with taking depositions of witnesses and employees of the defendant employer

- Produce to the defendants all of the pertinent data for the claim, such as medical bills, medical records, and tax returns

- Conduct a scheduling conference to set a trial date

- If necessary, obtain a 2nd opinion(IME- Independent Medical Examination) pursuant to Iowa Code § 85.39 to determine your permanent impairment rating, restrictions and to see if you need additional medical care and treatment

- Prepare a demand package to send to the defendant in attempt to settle the case

- Prepare for a possible mediation and/or settlement before trial

- Prepare for trial including organizing exhibits, etc.

- Organize the preparation of demonstrative exhibits for trial

- Prepare the client and witnesses for trial

- Take the case to trial before an administrative law judge

- Review and analyze the judge's decision to determine whether or not to appeal the case

- Make recommendations to the client as to whether or not to appeal the case[1]

---

[1] Our contract with you does not obligate us to participate in any appeal.

How Much is My Case Worth?

This is a question we often hear from clients during our initial interview. We tell our clients that every case is different and we cannot tell you how much your case is worth until we have all the facts. Be careful of attorneys who tell you that your case is worth $XXX,XXX before knowing all the facts in an effort to have you sign a fee contract. It is a dangerous practice, unreliable and can cause problems when it is time to try to settle your case. Sometimes doctors will change their opinions; factual witnesses are not able to be found, etc. Once we have gathered all the facts, conducted discovery, spoken with your doctors, and prepared a demand package then we will be able to discuss the value of your case.

Beware of the Medicare and Social Security Offset "Monsters"

You should be aware that if you have applied for or are currently receiving Social Security Disability benefits, there are special laws that apply to your case. You may be required to put a substantial portion of any settlement into a MSA- Medicare Set-Aside Trust to pay for future work related medical treatments. Also, there is special language that needs to be inserted into your settlement documents or your Social Security benefits can be "offset" which means reduced or eliminated which takes money out of your pocket. If these things are not taken into consideration and properly handled, an injured worker can lose much of a settlement.

The Legal Process in Workers' Compensation Cases

In many cases today, attempting to negotiate with the insurance company before filing a petition for arbitration (which is similar to filing a lawsuit in a civil case) is not worth the effort. Insurance companies often use the pre-suit negotiation only to attempt to find out as much about you, your attorney and your medical history as they can. Many attorneys waste precious time attempting to negotiate with the insurance company before filing a petition. If we accept your case it is because we believe that it has legal merit and that you deserve a trial if we are not able to reach a settlement. Often we will file your petition before negotiating so that if negotiations break down, we will already have a trial date in place to head towards. Please keep in mind that if we file a petition we will need to name as defendants your employer and their insurance company, if they are not self-insured.

It is a dangerous practice to wait until the last minute before the statute of limitations expires to file a petition. We have seen other attorneys do this only to find that the defendant they filed the petition against is not the correct defendant employer.

While there can be legitimate reasons for waiting to file a petition, there is no excuse for the practice that some attorneys use when they routinely wait until the last minute in hopes that the insurance company will settle your case. Unfortunately, we have also seen attorneys not licensed in Iowa attempt to represent people with claims in those jurisdictions. When the claims do not settle, they often panic to find an attorney to file the case on time. (We have received plenty of those last-minute calls for help, and we reject them because inaction is not going to be our crisis.). It is a dangerous practice for a client to hire an attorney who is not licensed in the jurisdiction where the petition must be filed.

Once the petition is filed, both sides engage in what is called discovery. Discovery is the process in which both sides "discover" what the evidence will be and what the other side will present at trial. The defendant will be permitted access to your medical records, work records and income tax returns. You will likely be required to give a deposition under oath and may be required to submit to a medical examination by a doctor hired by the defendant. We are also allowed to conduct discovery upon the defendant. The defendant will have to answer written questions called interrogatories, produce documents and be required to answer questions under oath in a deposition.

Can My Employer Fire Me?

This is a question we hear in almost every work injury case. Unfortunately, the general answer is "Yes". Iowa is an employee-at-will state, and the general rule is that your employer can fire you for any reason or no reason at all. However, there are some federal laws such as FMLA-Family Medical Leave Act and ADA- American with Disabilities Act which provide you with some protection. If you have an employment contract or are a member of a union subject to a collective bargaining agreement then you may have additional protection and may be able to file a grievance and keep your job. Finally, if you can prove that you were fired because you filed a workers' compensation claim or because of your age, sex, race, religion, etc. then you may have a separate employment law case.

(**WARNING:** THESE ARE GENERAL STATEMENTS AND ARE NOT INTENDED AS LEGAL ADVICE OR LEGAL OPINIONS. IF YOU THINK THAT YOU HAVE AN EMPLOYMENT LAW CLAIM THERE ARE DEADLINES WHICH CAN BE AS SHORT AS ONLY A FEW DAYS TO FILE A GRIEVANCE OR ONLY A FEW MONTHS TO FILE A COMPLAINT WITH THE CIVIL RIGHTS COMMISSION OR EQUAL EMPLOYMENT OPPORTUNITY COMMISSION. IF YOU THINK YOU HAVE AN EMPLOYMENT LAW CASE THEN YOU SHOULD CONSULT WITH AN ATTORNEY RIGHT AWAY.)

Page left blank intentionally.

Alternative Medical Care

What if the Insurance Company will not approve what their doctor recommends?

or

What if their doctors have nothing to offer me, and I find a doctor who says he/she can help?

There is a procedure known as a Petition for Alternative Medical Care (PAMC). This can be filed in an attempt to force the defendants to provide you with the care recommended by their doctors or to provide you with medical care from another doctor. Before filing a petition, you have to communicate your concerns with the insurance company (preferably in writing so there is no dispute about what you asked for) and request the medical care that you want by a certain date (usually 10 to 14 days is considered a reasonable amount of time). If they do not provide you with the care by that date, then you can file the Petition (Form 100C) which is available online at www.iowaworkforce.org/wc/publications.htm. It is a good idea to attach the applicable medical records that support your claim for alternative medical care to the petition.

If you have an attorney in your case, you should communicate your concerns regarding medical care to your attorney, and they can assist you through this process. Depending upon your injuries, you may not be able to find an attorney to take your case and may have to do this process on your own.

Please keep in mind that unlike an arbitration petition for benefits, the defendants can simply deny that your injuries are work related, and your (PAMC) will be dismissed. If the claim is denied and you have health insurance then you should be able to use your health insurance under Iowa Code § 85.38 to obtain medical care and treatment of your choice, but they will likely want to see the denial letter and documents before agreeing to pay for the bills. If you do not have health insurance then you should check into the Affordable Care Act or other government health insurance programs.

A (PAMC) is usually set for a telephone hearing within 2 to 3 weeks of filing, but if the defendants deny the claim then the hearing will be dismissed. At the hearing you can offer your exhibits attached to your petition. If you have additional evidence you should send it several days before the hearing and send a copy to the other side.

After hearing the evidence which usually consists of the injured worker testifying and perhaps someone from the defendants, the judge may rule immediately, but more likely will send out a written decision within 2 to 3 business days. However, they do have up to 10 business days to issue a decision. If either party does not like the judge's decision they can appeal the decision by seeking judicial review which is another detailed legal process that could be its own book.

Keep in mind that it is possible that the defendants will agree to provide the medical care or make an offer to provide what you are requesting or some other medical care at the time of or prior to the hearing.

How Can This Be Happening to Me?

Stories of Survival

How Karen Who Worked in a Factory Almost Lost $50,000

Take for example, Karen, one of our clients. Karen, was a 35 year old wife and mother of three working in the factory. Karen was a dependable worker who always came to work on time and had not missed a day of work in 4 years. Unfortunately, Karen was lifting a heavy part at work when her back gave-out. She ended up on the floor in severe pain. Karen immediately went to the medical office and reported that she had hurt her back at work. The medical personnel told her to go see her family doctor. Karen's family doctor prescribed pain medications and excused her from work for the next week. However, Karen's condition worsened and after only two days she was back seeing her family doctor. Her doctor ordered an MRI, which confirmed that Karen had suffered a herniated disc in her back. Karen was referred on to a surgeon for evaluation of the herniated disc. The surgeon told her that surgery was her best option as the disc would likely not heal on its own. Karen was devastated because she had never had surgery before and had always taken pride in her work.

While Karen had the surgery and made a good recovery, the doctor assigned her a 10% impairment rating and placed a permanent 30 pound lifting restriction upon her. She was not able to return to her higher paying line job, but had to take a lower paying job. She was satisfied with the 50 weeks of benefits they paid her, but did not realize that she was entitled to much more compensation for her injuries.

Thankfully, for Karen, one of her friends had previously been injured at his job, and we had handled his case for him. Karen came to see us, and we informed her that her case was worth much more than the 50 weeks of benefits she had been paid. She was entitled to industrial disability in which her impairment rating was only one of many factors. Karen eventually settled her case for more than twice as much as the insurance company had previously paid her. If Karen had not come to see us, she would have missed out on more than $50,000 in money owed to her.

How a Nurse Named Sharon
Almost Gave Away $200,000

Sharon is a nurse who injured her back while assisting a patient at work. She was a hard worker and seldom missed work before her injury. The insurance company for the hospital where she worked paid for her medical care including surgery and then made her an offer to settle based upon her impairment rating only. Sharon did not know how Iowa's workers' compensation laws worked so she requested a book that was offered at no cost to Iowans hurt at work. She read the book and learned that the impairment rating given to her by her doctor is only one factor in determining how much compensation she should receive. Her case eventually settled, but had she trusted her employer and their insurance company and taken their offer, she would have given away more than $200,000.

How an Insurance Company Tried to Cheat a Truck Driver Named Jim

Another client, Jim, was a hard working truck driver and father of two children. While he was driving his employer's tractor-trailer, he was involved in an accident causing him to sustain two broken bones in his back. He was immediately transported to the nearest trauma center where he spent the next several days. Doctors told Jim that he was lucky that he was not paralyzed, and a few days later he was released from the hospital and told to follow-up with his family doctor.

Jim notified his employer of the accident and the insurance company called him to take a statement. Jim told the insurance adjustor exactly what happened, and a few days later he received a letter stating that they were denying his claim and not paying his lost wages or medical expenses. Jim was desperate when he called our office as he was not receiving any income. We did some checking up. We obtained the accident report, hired a private investigator and contacted the insurance company about their previous decision. Once we intervened in the case, the insurance company decided that Jim's claim was legitimate and began paying him for his lost wages. After missing several months of work, Jim made a satisfactory recovery, and we were able to obtain a "just" settlement for him.

Why Should You Consider Hiring Us?

As we said at the beginning of this book, "we are not your average Iowa attorneys." Instead of running around trying to manage hundreds of cases at a time, we carefully select the few cases that we will accept at any one time.

There are many attorneys who advertise for work injury cases. Unfortunately, some of these attorneys have so many small cases in their offices that no case gets their personal attention. Others have no real intention of trying your case themselves, and if the case cannot be settled with the insurance company, they will refer the case out for trial. Many will not even bother to talk with your doctors until they ask for their opinions for the first time during a deposition. There are good experienced attorneys in this field, but it can be very difficult for a consumer to separate the good from the bad.

PERSONAL ATTENTION

Our clients get personal attention because we are very selective in the cases that we take. We decline dozens of cases each year in order to devote personal, careful attention to those that we accept. We take the time and spend the money to go meet with your doctors and explain to them how they can assist in your case. We prepare every case like it is going to trial because we do not know which ones will need to be tried until the end. Also, we offer our unique Injured Iowans First Fee Schedule™.

What Cases We Generally Do Not Accept?

Due to the very high volume of calls and referrals from other attorneys that we receive, we have found that the only way to provide personal service is to decline those cases that do not meet our strict criteria. Therefore, we generally do not accept the following types of cases:

☐ Cases involving scheduled member only injuries such as fingers, hands, arms and legs. Our experience is that many injured workers can handle their own scheduled member injury cases. Therefore, we believe that our time is better spent helping those with other cases. However, we do accept scheduled member injury cases if you have been diagnosed with CRPS- Chronic Regional Pain Syndrome, RSD- Reflex Sympathetic Dystrophy or another nerve injury. Also, if you have a prior injury to a scheduled member, whether it is work related or not, you may be entitled to 2nd injury fund benefits and we do accept those cases. If you wonder if we will take your case, please call us and we will let you know. If we do not take your case then we will refer you to someone who may.

☐ If you are done treating for an unscheduled member injury such as your back, shoulder, neck or brain injury and you have returned to your job making the same wages and you do not have either a permanent impairment rating or permanent restrictions. We would like to represent everyone who needs a good attorney, but we cannot. If you have a question about this, contact us and we can help you figure it out.

☐ Cases where the statute of limitations will soon run-out. We like to have at least 2 months to adequately investigate and evaluate your claim. Your delay is not going to become our crisis taking away from our other clients.

☐ If a petition has already been filed by another attorney, we will not represent you. We like to do things our way. If another attorney has already filed the petition, that's fine, but we will not handle your case.

Well, Are There Any Cases Left?

Yes, there are, and that is the point because with hard work and personal attention we **Level the Field** Between **Injured Iowans and Insurance Companies**™ by **Fighting for Justice and Respect.**™

"We Concentrate our Efforts on Increasing the Value of the Good Cases—

We represent many clients with significant valid claims. When we devote our time and resources to representing only legitimate claimants with good claims, we are able to do our best work. We have found that spending countless hours on lots of little cases, each with a "unique problem," is not good for our other clients.

Why Consider Hiring Attorneys From Central Iowa?

The Iowa Workers' Compensation Commission is located in Des Moines, Iowa. The judges have offices there, and there are 3 hearing rooms in Des Moines. Yes, there are other places where hearings are held, but generally it takes longer to obtain a hearing date in one of the other locations which include Cedar Rapids, Council Bluffs, Davenport, Iowa Falls, Ottumwa, Sioux City and Waterloo. Also, in the locations outside of Des Moines, you receive both a primary and back-up hearing date which means sometimes you will not know until the night before the hearing if your case will be heard the next day. The location of your hearing is determined by where you were injured, but if the parties agree, the hearing can be scheduled in Des Moines.

We feel that Des Moines is the best location to have a hearing for several reasons. The judges who have hearings in locations outside of Des Moines are staying in a hotel and may be scheduled to hear 3 or more cases each day for 3 or more days in a row. You can imagine how you would feel sleeping in a strange bed and location working very hard every day. It seems to us that the judges are more relaxed and prefer to have hearings in Des Moines where they live.

We have offices in Des Moines, Newton, Ankeny and Marshalltown, but we represent clients from all over the state and often meet with them near their home. Almost everything in the case can be done through mail, telephone or email if you use email. If your case is scheduled to be heard in Des Moines, then chances are the only times you will be required to travel to Des Moines is for your hearing (if your case is not settled) and perhaps for your deposition.

Page left blank intentionally.

WHAT ARE SOME CRITICAL THINGS TO REMEMBER WHEN DEALING WITH A WORK INJURY?

7 DEADLY MISTAKES TO AVOID IF YOU ARE HURT AT WORK

Here is what we consider to be the Seven Secrets to Not Get Hurt Again by Your Work Injury case. These secrets are based upon our experience and discussions with many judges and other attorneys.

1. NOT REPORTING YOUR WORK INJURY- Iowa law requires that you report a work injury within 90 days of when you knew or should have known you were injured at work. For example, if you go to your family doctor with an injury you think might be work related and your doctor confirms that it is work related, then notify your employer immediately.

2. FAILING TO GO TO THE DOCTOR EVEN THOUGH YOU ARE INJURED- If you have been injured and are having medical problems then you need to go to the doctor. If you fail to go to the doctor then the insurance company will use it against you because they will say if you did not go to the doctor then you must not have been hurt.

3. NOT TELLING THE DOCTOR EVERYTHING THAT HURTS AND UNDERSTATING YOUR INJURIES- Perhaps you are having pain and numbness in your hands, but have also been having problems with your shoulder or neck. While your hands may be the focus of your examination, make sure to write down on the forms and tell the doctor about all of your medical problems related to

your work injury. Also, if you tell the doctor and/or other medical providers including physical therapists, etc. that you are all right or are fine when you are really still having problems, then the doctor and/or therapist will write in your medical records that you are back to normal. It is important that you tell the doctor and/or other medical providers if you are still having pain, limitation, etc.

Along the same lines, it is usually best to not write letters to your doctors or request opinion letters from them. Leave it up to your attorney to do this as he or she should have the experience to provide the necessary information to your doctor. Also, any letters that you write to a medical provider will likely be kept in your file and later on your employer and/or their insurance company may use it against you.

4. FAILING TO FOLLOW-UP WITH MEDICAL CARE AND GAPS IN TREATMENT- Failing to see a physician regularly is considered evidence that you have fully recovered to the insurance company and eventually, perhaps to the judge deciding your case. While you should not go to the doctor every day, you need to see your doctors and tell them if you are still having problems. If your doctor says "follow-up as needed", that means to come back in a few weeks if you are still having problems. If you do not follow-up, then in the eyes of the doctor, insurance company, and jury, you are no longer having problems and have made a full recovery.

5. BE CAREFUL WHAT YOU SAY AND DO: The insurance company and their lawyers will use anything and everything they can against you. Even a small lie or exaggeration can hurt your credibility so the best policy is to always tell the truth. Nowadays, the Internet, Facebook and other social media sites can damage your case. We

recommend to our clients that they disable, but do not destroy, all social media sites that they have while their injury matter is pending. We recommend this because if a claim is filed, you will probably be required to provide Facebook and other social media pages to the other side in your case. For example, if pictures are posted of you smiling and having a good time after an injury, the defense attorney will show the judge or jury the picture and argue, "Does this person asking for money look like they are in pain and cannot work"? While the picture may be a short time period where you were living your life, it can damage your credibility and your case.

Along the same lines, **DO NOT MISREPRESENT YOUR ACTIVITY LEVEL:** Insurance companies routinely hire private investigators to conduct videotape surveillance. If you claim that you cannot run, climb or stoop, and you get caught on videotape doing these things it can be very damaging to your case.

Also, you will often be asked to rate your pain on a scale of 1 to 10. While the pain scale is not usually explained to you, please understand that according to the pain scale, if you had pain at the level 8 to 10 you would be screaming with pain and most likely be in a hospital. Please keep this in mind while answering the pain scale questions.

6. FAILING TO REPORT FOR WORK AFTER BEING RELEASED- If the employer's doctor or your own doctor tells you that you can return to work with restrictions, you need to go to work and make yourself available for work within your restrictions. If you do not report for work, then workers' compensation will not pay you and even worse, you may be fired.

7. ACCEPTING WHAT THE INSURANCE COMPANY PAYS YOU- Often times the insurance company will pay you money consisting of your impairment rating <u>only</u>. The insurance company should pay you your impairment rating **without requiring you to sign** settlement documents. If you have an injury to an unscheduled member (such as an injury to your back, shoulder, neck, brain, etc.) then the impairment rating may only be a small portion of what you are owed. Further, even if you have a scheduled member injury (hand, arm, leg, foot or eye) you may be entitled to additional benefits from the 2nd injury fund. Sometimes the insurance company will offer additional money for a "closed file" or "compromise settlement". Be wary of a settlement offered by insurance company because it may be far below the fair value of your case claim and will likely eliminate your future medical care and claims for future benefits.

OUR CASES, VERDICTS AND RESULTS

Here are some cases that we have successfully resolved. There are others at our website at www.IowaInjured.com. Remember that each case is different. Once a case is in the hands of a judge, it is out of our control. We have had cases in which we were pleasantly surprised by the verdict and others in which we were disappointed. We do not win every case, and sometimes we obtain a verdict that we are not able to collect the money owed from the defendant due to lack of insurance or other reasons. However, we do believe that significant trial experience and results are factors that people may use to choose one attorney over another. With these things in mind, here are some of our results which are the total amount received before the deduction of attorney fees and costs:

$310,000 Settlement for Truck Driver with Back Injury

An over the road truck driver injured his back while switching trailers. He had 2 back surgeries and sustained significant permanent restrictions. A settlement of $310,000 was reached in mediation with the driver's employer.

Judge Finds Nurse Permanently and Totally Disabled, Expected Payments of More Than $800,000

A verdict of permanent total disability was entered for a nurse providing her with weekly benefits and medical care for the rest of her life resulting in expected payments of more than $800,000.

$335,000 Settlement for Police Officer

A police officer from Eastern Iowa sustained multiple injuries (shoulder replacement, tinnitus, balance disorder, etc.) when he was struck by a fleeing suspect. During a mediation his case was settled for $335,000, plus ongoing medical care for his work injuries.

Judge Finds Woman to have 40% Disability Following a Shoulder Injury with Surgery

A woman from Northern Iowa sustained a shoulder injury which required surgery at work. She proceeded to trial and the judge determined she sustained 40% disability resulting in more than $60,000 in benefits to be paid.

Factory Worker Receives a Lifetime of Workers' Compensation Benefits Estimated to be Worth More than $300,000

A lifetime of weekly workers' compensation benefits (estimated to be worth more than $300,000) was ordered to be paid by an Iowa Workers' compensation judge. The benefits are being paid by the Iowa Second Injury Fund for a wrist injury requiring fusion surgery which was sustained by the injured worker at Kinze Manufacturing in Williamsburg, Iowa.

$120,000 Settlement After Trial and Appeal for Clerical Worker

After a trial followed by an appeal, a settlement of $120,000 was reached for a clerical worker who sustained injuries to both of her arms requiring multiple surgeries.

$180,000 Settlement for Computer Technician with Back and Neck Injuries

A computer technician was involved in a single car accident while returning from a job back to the airport. He lost control of his rental car causing it to roll into a ditch. While his back and neck injuries did not require surgery, they did prevent him from doing many things that he did prior to his work injury. Through the use of mediation we were able to resolve his case for $180,000, plus the insurance company agreed to pay to set-up a MSA-Medicare Set-Aside Trust because he had applied for Social Security disability benefits.

$200,000 Settlement for Factory Worker with Neck and Shoulder Injuries

A local factory worked had sustained neck and shoulder injuries during the course of her 15 year work history. While she had physical therapy and prescription medications to treat these conditions nothing seemed to help. While the doctors did not have a surgery to fix her problems she was left with physical limitations which prevented her from returning to the factory. We were able to successfully resolve her case while preserving her health insurance benefits with her employer.

60% Disability Provided to Worker Who Sustained (2nd Injury) to Leg

A worker who had previously sustained an injury to his left leg sustained a 2nd work related injury to his right leg which resulted in him qualifying for Social Security Disability benefits. The judge determined that the worker sustained 60% industrial disability, and he will be paid a total of 300 weeks of benefits totaling more than $130,000.

$125,000 Settlement for Factory Worker with an Arm Injury

A settlement of $125,000 was reached for a factory worker who was not called back to work after a work related arm injury requiring surgery resulting in permanent restrictions.

Jailer to Receive a Lifetime of Benefits Worth More than $375,000 for an Eye Injury

A judge ordered a Clarke County jailer to receive a weekly workers' compensation check for the rest of her life due to an eye injury worth more than $375,000. She had previously sustained injuries to her hands which qualified her for Iowa Second Injury Fund benefits.

$120,000 Settlement for Worker Who Fell

A settlement of $120,000 was obtained for a man who fell at work sustaining a broken bone causing permanent medical problems.

What Do Our Past Clients Have to Say?
<u>TESTIMONIALS</u>

We represented hundreds of clients, and the vast majority of them have been happy with our legal services. Remember that each case is different and past results are not a guarantee that you will be happy with our services. With this being said, here is what some of our past clients have to say. In order to preserve confidentiality, only their first names and location are listed. There are others at our website at www.IowaInjured.com.

I had never called an attorney's office before and now I'm very glad I did. Corey Walker and his staff treated me with respect from the very beginning. I felt very comfortable from the first time I talked to him. Corey showed me that there are still people who care about other people and fight for our rights. I would have never received a dime if it wasn't for Corey. I will recommend his law firm to anyone. Also, the secretaries were big help and very respectful to me. Thank you and once again, you have brought back my faith in the system.

Robin of Hardin County (Factory worker)

Mr. Bair was more than my attorney in this matter – he was a friend. In today's society of rush, rush, he took the time to listen to my problems and concerns. This was very stressful times for myself and knowingly Erik would just call just to ask if there were any questions I had during this process, that's a true friend. I will highly recommend Walker, Billingsley & Bair to all my family and friends! Again thank you from my family.

Tim of Des Moines (Warehouse worker)

I was injured at a nursing job I had worked at for more than 20 years. Because of my injuries, I could not return to my previous job. I talked to several attorneys about handling my case, but then I met with Corey. He took the time to answer my questions and explain all the aspects of my case. I am glad I chose Corey because he was able to obtain a fair settlement in my case and now I can move on with my life.

Kathy of Marshalltown (RN- Registered Nurse)

I felt very comfortable talking with Corey and his staff about my case and experiences. My wife and I couldn't imagine having a more professional and successful outcome with any other attorney. I was concerned that Iowa was a right to work state and I didn't know what rights I had if any. I was worried distance may be a problem but Corey's cooperation made things go very smoothly. Corey was very informative about rights and laws that I had no idea existed and improved my outcome considerably.

Greg of Sioux City (Maintenance worker)

I could not have asked for a better attorney that I have had in Corey Walker. I was lost when I contacted him for my work comp case and he took care of everything. It was a great feeling to know I was not facing this whole ordeal alone.

Gail of Council Bluffs, Iowa (Housekeeper at hotel)

When I came to Corey, I did not even know I had a case against the Second Injury Fund of Iowa. I only thought I had a case against my employer and their insurance company. The Second Injury Fund did not want to pay what the case was worth, so went to trial. While it did take some time to receive compensation, once I did, the ruling was for much more than I had expected. I would strongly recommend that others use Corey as an attorney in their workers' compensation cases. You may have a Second Injury Fund case and not even know it. If I had not called Corey about my workers' compensation case, I would have lost out on more than $100,000.

Bill of Polk County, Iowa (Truck driver)

Mr. Bair was very helpful in my case and he was very respectful. He contacted me about concerns for my case and kept me updated. I would recommend Erik to all my friends or relatives that would be looking for an attorney. I've enjoyed reading the monthly newsletter I hope I can continue to receive one in the mail. I want to say thank you Mr. Bair you went out of your way to help me.

Rene of Madrid, Iowa (Farm worker)

I want to thank Attorney Grife for her hard and dedicated work on my behalf. I truly feel she went above and beyond the norm to win my litigation case. I also know she is a superb attorney, whom if needed I will recommend and call on again. My deepest gratitude goes out to her and her associates. It is nice to know you are represented by such a quality attorney. Thank you Mrs. Grife!

Rodney, of Clinton, Iowa (Store clerk)

While working as a nurse at a Des Moines hospital, I fell injuring my back. While I was able to complete my shift, my back has never been the same. I have not been able to return to work and may never be able to work again. I saw a small ad that attorney Corey Walker put in the newspaper offering a free work injury book. I called to request the book to find out more about work injuries and my rights.

After reading his book, my husband and I met with Corey and he took my case. He did not charge me anything while my case was pending for several years. The doctors have told me that there is no surgery that will fix my back, but I know that with Corey's help I will now be able to provide for my family even though I may never work again.

January of Polk County, Iowa (Nurse)

I sustained work injuries to my knees which prevented me from returning to my job. I called Corey's office and he sent me some materials explaining my rights. Then I went to see Corey who took my case with no money down and we went to trial where we won. When I came to him, I did not even know I had a case against the Iowa Second Injury Fund. I only thought I had a case against my employer and their insurance company. I strongly recommend that others use Corey as an attorney for their workers' compensation case. You may have an Iowa Second Injury Fund case and not even know it. If I had not called Corey, I would have lost out on more than $120,000. If you have sustained a work injury then go talk to Corey because he will not give-up and will fight for you to until the end.

Jackie of Victor, Iowa (Copier repair person)

I sustained an injury and the insurance company offered to settle my case. I suspected that their offer was too low and when I went to see Corey Walker, I was right. Corey helped me with my case and quickly obtained me the settlement that I deserved.

Randy of Boone, Iowa (Factory worker)

From start to finish everything was handled perfectly. I couldn't be more happy. I received more than I expected. Joanie is a great attorney and works for a fantastic firm. Thanks to the entire staff at Walker, Billingsley & Bair! I will refer you to others in need of help! If I need any future legal help I will be contacting you guys. I'll stick with the law firm that has proven itself to me.

Larry of Eldora (Production worker)

I hurt my back while working construction which is all I have ever done. Because of my back injury, I could not go back to working construction and was left with filing for workers' compensation and Social Security disability. Corey was able to negotiate a settlement which allowed me to keep my monthly Social Security disability benefits and receive a lump-sum settlement for my work injury. If I had not hired Corey, I would have lost almost 50% of my monthly Social Security benefits because of the Social Security disability offset. Corey saved me thousands of dollars of lost benefits and obtained a good settlement for me. If you have been injured at work and are considering filing for Social Security disability you should go talk to Corey. With his experience and hard work he will protect you and your rights.

Butch of Tama, Iowa (Construction worker)

Erik was outstanding and patient, a very good person and I thank him a lot.

Robert of Des Moines, Iowa (School Custodian)

I hurt my shoulder at work and because of my injury, I could no longer do many of the jobs that I had done in the past. The insurance company made me an offer to settle my case. I had no idea if the offer was fair or not so I went to see Corey for a free consultation and audit of my case. He told me that the offer was too low and he filed a petition for benefits. If the insurance company makes an offer in your workers' compensation case, you should go see Corey. I am glad I did because with his hard work I received $25,000 more than the insurance company offered me before hiring Corey.

Gregg of Newton, Iowa (Maintenance worker)

I hurt my neck while working for a local company. Even though I had to have neck surgery, my employer and their insurance company denied that my neck injury was caused by work. I saw an ad for a free book about work injuries so I called and got the book. After reading his book, I hoped that Corey would help me with my case. Corey agreed to meet with me at no charge. At our meeting, he agreed to help me. He got my medical records and then had a conference with my surgeon to prove that my neck injury was work related. While the insurance company would not admit that my injury was work related, with Corey's help I was able to get a good settlement. If the insurance company denies that your injury is work related you should give Corey a call. If I had not called Corey I would have given-up thousands of dollars.

John of Story County, Iowa (Sanitation worker)

Excellent job to all and thank you so much Siobhan for all the talks. 100% satisfied.

Richard of Newton, Iowa (Mechanic)

I worked at a hospital and fell in the parking lot on some ice. In the fall I injured my back, but the doctors told me that there was no surgery to fix it. My back pain became so severe that I could no longer do my job which required a lot of sitting along with bending over and retrieving files. The insurance company refused to provide additional treatment for my back injury so I went to see Corey. Corey went to meet with my doctors and was able to prove to the insurance company that my back injury was caused by my fall at work. He got my medical treatment started again and then got me a good settlement through mediation. I appreciate his dedication and hard work on my case.

Cindy of Altoona, Iowa (Billing clerk)

Totally satisfied with everything and how it was handled. I was referred to Corey by a coworker and a relative and it was the best decision I made. Thank you very much for your services.

Larry of New Sharon, Iowa (Electrical engineer)

Corey, you are my saving hero. The settlement you obtained for me after my back injury is what has kept me from 'going under' financially. There are not enough words to adequately express my appreciation for your excellent work on my behalf.

Gwen Duff of Scranton, IA (Nurse)

I would encourage anyone to hire an attorney from Walker, Billingsley & Bair Law Firm. My experience with your firm was outstanding. I wouldn't change anything. My phone calls and emails were always returned in a timely manner. Whenever I called the office the staff was always nice and pleasant and assisted me with the questions I had.

Quinten of Williamsburg, Iowa (Factory worker)

When the workers' compensation insurance company stopped paying me benefits for my shoulder injury, I went to see attorney Corey Walker. He handled my workers' compensation case in a professional and aggressive manner. He timely returned my phone calls and kept me informed of what was going on with my case. While it did take some time, he made the insurance company accept responsibility for my work injury and pay me fair compensation. If you have been hurt at work and are not being treated fairly, go talk to Corey because he will fight hard for your rights.

Lindsay of Knoxville, Iowa (Ambulance personnel)

I hurt my back when I fell in the factory. I went through physical therapy, but I still had problems. While I was able to return to work and do my job, I was eventually fired by the company. Despite losing my job, the insurance company did not offer to pay me any permanent benefits so I went to see Corey. Corey filed a workers' compensation petition for me and was able to get me a good settlement before the trial. If I had not gone to see Corey then I would not have received any money for my back injury. If you have been hurt at work and are still having problems then go see Corey.

Wane of Newton, Iowa (Factory worker)

I was injured on the job when I fell from a roof sustaining severe and permanent injuries. The insurance company stopped making workers' compensation payments which I suspected was not right. I requested some information from Corey which he sent to me right away. Then I went to see him and he explained to me that the insurance company should not have stopped my benefits. He contacted the insurance company right away and my weekly benefits started again. He then filed a claim on my behalf and we were able to settle the case. If the insurance company stops your benefits, then you should go see Corey because you may be entitled to additional compensation.

Don of Ft. Dodge, Iowa (Roofer)

Siobhan Schneider was good to me. Friendly and understanding, always explained what was going on with the case, always returned phone calls. I didn't think I could get more money but your firm did me good.

LaVonne of Dubuque (Delivery driver)

I was hurt on the job breaking bones in my leg. The insurance company started paying me benefits, but then stopped and would not return my phone calls. I went to see Corey who explained to me the Iowa Workers' Compensation laws. He pursued my case and the insurance company paid the benefits they owed, plus interest. If you are hurt at work and the insurance company stops your benefits you should call Corey.

Andrew of Newton, Iowa (Construction worker)

I greatly appreciated the support I got from Corey. He is an awesome attorney and person. He stood by me the whole time and I put my sole trust in him. He did not let me down. Thank you very much.

Deb of New Sharon (Store clerk)

Thank you very much for helping me get through this claim and being a listening post, I couldn't have done it without your help. I appreciated your kindness and help, again I thank you.

Sheila of Pleasantville, Iowa (Production worker)

Our Services

We are here to provide you with personal service and protect your rights throughout your case. Sometimes the best advice we can give is that you do not have a claim that can be won. If that is true, we will tell you so. If your case meets our criteria and we decide to accept your case, you will receive our personal attention. We provide you with copies of letters written and let you know what the current status is of your case. We will give you our advice as to whether your case should be settled or if we should proceed to trial where one of us will be trying your case. Also, if you ever have any questions please feel free to contact us. We would rather have you call and ask us your questions rather than sit and wonder what the answer is. We are committed to providing the attention to details and personal service that Injured Iowans deserve.

For the cases that qualify, we offer a *no cost, no obligation* audit and review of your case. We will fully explain all fees and costs to you before proceeding. Together, as a team, we will decide on the best tactics for your case.

Corey J. L. Walker, Erik D. Bair,
Siobhan Schneider & Joanie L. Grife

WHAT IS OUR GUARANTEE TO YOU?

We will invest our time, resources and abilities into your case. We will even share the risk of success with you because in most cases we advance all of the initial costs for your case. Because of this, you will be able to get your case started without paying any money out of your pocket.

This is our guarantee of commitment to you!!

What About Car and Motorcycle Accidents, Dog Bites, Medical Negligence/Malpractice, Falls, Product Liability and Wrongful Death?

Whenever you are hurt by anyone's negligence, including that of another driver, dog owner, medical provider, store merchant or manufacturer you have a "personal injury" claim. Car and truck accidents (injuries caused by a negligent driver), dog bites (injuries caused by a dog or other animal), medical malpractice or negligence (injuries caused by a medical mistake), falls (injury because someone did not take care of the walkway for example), product liability (injury by harmful product) and wrongful death (where a loved one is killed in a personal injury accident) are all subtypes of personal injury cases. We also handle these specialized personal injury cases and have a special book about them. To request the book called "Iowa Car Accidents, Personal Injury and Wrongful Death- A Comprehensive Consumer Survival Guide to Iowa Injuries" call toll free at 1-888-829-3393 or log on to www.IowaInjuryBook.com.

Page left blank intentionally.

Special Report

Injured Iowans First Fee Schedule ™

A new approach of determining attorney fees in work injury claims!

Should an attorney charge the same percentage whether they spend 2 hours or 2 years on a case?

(Of Course Not)

Corey J. L. Walker, Erik D. Bair, Siobhan Schneider & Joanie L. Grife
Iowa Workers' Compensation Attorneys

Walker, Billingsley & Bair

Ankeny **2605 SW White Birch, Ste. 110- 515-964-5664**
Des Moines- 2545 E. Euclid, Ste. 120- 515-440-2852
Marshalltown- 25 North Center St.- 641-352-4747
Newton- 208 N. 2nd Ave. West- 641-792-3595

www.IowaWorkInjury.com
Corey@IowaInjured.com

Our Injured Iowans First Fee Schedule™ in Work Injury Cases

Attorneys should charge reasonable fees based upon:

- The amount of time involved and the results obtained
- The novelty and difficulty of the questions involved and the skill required by the attorney to properly represent the client
- The desires and goals of the client

We have developed a revolutionary and progressive Injured Iowans First Fee Schedule™ for our work injury clients. First of all, if you are currently receiving weekly benefits we do not take a fee on those benefits. Also, if the treating authorized physician determines that you have permanent impairment rating and the insurance company or employer voluntarily pays that impairment rating we do not take a fee on those benefits.

While we believe that many insurance companies will not make their best offer until we hold their feet to the fire on the eve of trial, we understand that clients have different wants and needs from a work injury claim. If the attorney fees are less than the "standard fee", then the client may be able to settle his or her case sooner and still end up with the same amount of money in his or her pocket instead of waiting a year or more for a trial. While an insurance company may not be willing to pay top dollar early in the case, because the attorney is not charging the standard fee early in this case, the client may choose to accept a lower amount from the insurance company. In fact, there are some cases where a percentage fee may not be the best choice. For example, in a case with a prior offer, the client may want to pay an hourly fee to the attorney which may save the client thousands of dollars in the process! This is why we developed the **Injured Iowans First Fee Schedule ™** in work injury and personal injury cases.

INJURED IOWANS FIRST FEE SCHEDULE™

Contingent Fee

Our **Injured Iowans First Fee Schedule™** means that the earlier your case is resolved, the lower our attorney fee percentage is. This may enable you to accept a lower settlement from the insurance company, but still come out ahead. If you tell us to, we will even advise the insurance company of our lower fee which may encourage them to make a reasonable offer to you earlier rather than later.

Also, there is <u>no risk to you</u> because you do not owe us anything, unless we are able to recover more than the treating authorized physician's permanent impairment rating. If we are able to recover more than the treating authorized physician's permanent impairment rating then our fee is a percentage of the additional recovery depending on how far the case goes. If your case is settled before filing a petition our percentage is lower than if we have to file a petition. If we file a petition and have a trial our percentage is lower than if we have a trial and there is an appeal.[2]

---

[2] (**NOTICE**: WE ARE NOT OBLIGATED TO APPEAL YOUR CASE AND CONTINGENCY FEES ARE PAID ON THE TOTAL RECOVERY AND ARE COMPUTED BEFORE DEDUCTING EXPENSES.)

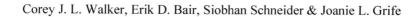

Page left blank intentionally.

No Cost Subscription Offer

Would you like to know:
- · How to avoid insurance company denials;
- · How to protect you and your family from financial ruin;
- · Legal Insider Secrets about Iowa's laws;
- · How current legal issues and cases which may affect you;
- · The "inside story" about frivolous lawsuits;
- · Practical advice about buying insurance from someone who does not sell insurance;
- · What you must do if you are hurt at work.

These are some of the topics covered in a newsletter entitled "**The Iowa Legal Insider**" sent to your home each month at no cost by Iowa Work Injury Attorney Corey Walker and Walker, Billingsley & Bair. Mr. Walker understands and believes that most legal disputes could be avoided if people knew more about the legal system.

There is absolutely no cost or obligation, and we routinely have drawings to win race tickets to the Iowa Speedway, Richard Petty Driving School Ride-Alongs, etc. If you subscribe and later feel like we are wasting your time, there is a phone number and an email address in every issue that you can contact to cancel. Don't worry, these are not the boring, "canned" newsletters that most firms buy and slap their name on to. We write it and we aim to provoke people to pay more attention to their legal affairs.

There is no need to destroy this book. Just photocopy this form and fill it out. Also, feel free to make extra copies to give to friends or family that may be interested. You can mail it to Corey Walker 208 N. 2nd Ave. West Newton, Iowa 50208; Fax it to 641-792-0289; or email the information below to Corey@IowaInjured.com. Please start my no cost subscription:

Name: _____

Address: _____

City:_____ State: _____ Zip: _____

Email: _____@_____

We do not share our mail/email lists with anyone!

87

The
Haystacks
Church

Andy Nash

iR

REVIEW AND HERALD® PUBLISHING ASSOCIATION

Since 1861 | www.reviewandherald.com

This book was
Edited by Gerald Wheeler
Copyedited by Megan Mason
Cover Designed by Bryan Gray / Review and Herald® Design Center
Interior Designed by Emily Ford / Review and Herald® Design Center
Cover art by
Typeset: Minion Pro 11/13

PRINTED IN U.S.A.
16 15 14 13 12   5 4 3 2 1

Library of Congress Cataloging-in-Publication Data
Nash, Andy, 1971-   .
  The haystacks church / Andy Nash.
     p. cm.
  1. Adventists—Doctrines. I. Title.
  BX6121.N37 2012
  286.7'32—dc23
                                 2012040292
ISBN 978-0-8280-2698-7

Dedication

To William Johnsson, who showed me both grace and truth.

Contents

Part 3: Being Adventist

Part 4: Advent

Introduction

The Haystacks Church

Fifteen years ago I wrote a book called *Growing Up Adventist*. In one of my stories from my childhood I told about a crisis at a church potluck: attempting to eat a taco for the first time.

"Every time I tried to take a bite," I wrote, "the shell cracked a little more. My taco was quickly collapsing. Tomatoes, lettuce, and sour cream oozed onto my plate while my friends threw down their napkins and bolted off to the dessert bar. I wept.

"Dad looked down the table at his son sobbing over a taco. It couldn't have been one of his prouder moments. 'Tacos are kind of tricky to eat, aren't they, pal?' he said.

" 'Mm-hmm,' I whimpered.

" 'But,' he said, 'haystacks are much easier.'

" 'What do you mean?' I asked

"Taking a fork, Dad crushed my taco shell and spread the contents evenly around my plate. 'There,' he said. 'Now you have a haystack, and no one else does.'

"Seconds later I was scooping up my haystack—which no one else had—and hoping that someday I'd be as smart as Dad."

A lot can change in 15 years. Now I'm a dad, and our kids come to Cindy and me with the broken tacos of life. Truth be told, we still experience a few ourselves. I imagine you do too.

Maybe that's why haystacks are such a fitting symbol for our church. Again and again God has turned the disappointments, the brokenness, of this faith community into something worth salvaging as we await the return of our Savior, Jesus Christ.

This book isn't about growing up Adventist—it's about being Adventist. Whether you're a lifelong Adventist, a new church member, or an interested onlooker, I hope you'll enjoy this conversation around the potluck table.

—Andy Nash

Part 1

Why
Be Adventist?

Chapter 1

The Treasure House

Imagine that one morning you're walking alongside a quiet road when suddenly you come upon an ancient stone house. Drawing closer, you notice that the front door of the house has swung open, apparently from a breeze. Curious, you decide to take a look inside.

As you enter the doorway, you see two large rooms—one to the left, the other to the right. A wall separates the rooms. No one else is here.

You take a few cautious steps to the left, and within moments you can't believe what you're seeing. The room is full of ancient treasure. *Biblical* treasure. You recognize it immediately: golden lamp stands, silver cups, scrolls made of animal skins. And there—right there in the center of the room—is the biggest treasure of all: the holy ark of the covenant! How can this be?

Approaching the ark, you eye its construction of acacia wood overlaid with gold. Two golden angels face each other, their wings nearly touching, their eyes gazing downward. You follow their eyes to the opened ark, and, leaning forward, you peer in.

Two stone tablets lay side by side. They match: two copies of the same covenant, one for God, one for His people.

As you stand in this treasure room, trying to take it all in, you hear the front door swing open again. *Why is it doing that?* you wonder.

Retracing your steps, you walk back to the doorway—and then to the room you haven't yet seen. As you come around the corner, your hands go cold.

It is full of treasure too, but of a different type: a smaller collection of parchments, a basin and towel, a jar of nard perfume—each resting at the foot of a large, crude wooden cross.

For a long time you stand in this room.

Suddenly you hear something outside. Voices. Rushing to the doorway, you reach it in time to see a multitude approaching the house. They enter and file past you, some to the left, others to the right. Clearly the people have been here before—they know their way around.

You follow the group to the first room. They are studying the treasure: unrolling the scrolls, touching the lamp stands, peering into the ark, animatedly discussing everything they're seeing. Then you return to the second room. Here too the people stand around marveling at the treasure. Some of them have fallen facedown among it.

What strikes you is how loyal each group is to their respective room. Some do cross over and visit the other room, almost with an air of novelty. But without question, both groups have their own comfort zone.

What you keep coming back to is this breeze. Is it just your imagination, or is it getting stronger and stronger—like a full-blown wind? The door strains harder and harder at its hinges. Even the walls themselves seem ready to shake. Then somewhere you hear the fluttering of pages . . .

Chapter 2

One Friday Evening

I'll never forget my first Friday evening in Jerusalem—and the surprising clarity it brought to my Seventh-day Adventist faith.

It had been my lifelong dream to visit Israel, and at age 37 I'd finally got the opportunity. My traveling partners were an 8-year-old and a 10-year-old: my daughters Ally and Morgan. My wife, Cindy, had visited Israel before, so she stayed home with our youngest daughter, Summer, who wasn't very happy about it.

Earlier that warm June day the girls and I'd taken a break from our touring to go swimming at a public pool I'd managed to locate in my guidebook. We'd been seeing sights for several days now, and the girls had needed a breather. Maybe their dad had too. As they'd splashed in the pool with a dozen Israeli children, I'd thought about how special the little trip had already been for us.

After an overnight flight, we'd spent our first day shaking off jet lag at the Mediterranean Sea. For hours we'd bodysurfed just down the shore from the biblical town of Joppa—where Jonah had famously set sail. As we'd rode the waves, the girls and I had teased each other about spotting whales nearby. "I'm serious!" we'd take turns shouting. "I really see one this time!"

The next morning we'd journeyed up to Jerusalem, as had so many before us: Abraham and Isaac, David and Solomon, Ezra and Nehemiah, Mary and Joseph. When we'd stepped from the taxi into history, I'd never seen my daughters' eyes so wide. Hand in tight hand, the three of us had woven through narrow streets, taking in places that had previously existed only in our Bibles: the Mount of Olives, Gethsemane, the upper room.

Late that evening we'd arrived at the massive Church of the Holy Sepulcher, the traditional site of Jesus' tomb. The dark corridors of the church had confused us, and after several left turns in a row, we'd just stood still, utterly lost. In front of us had been some type of shrine with candles at its entrance. A lone traveler had walked by.

"Excuse me," I'd said. "What is that?"

"That," he'd said slowly, "is the sepulcher of Christ."

What? I'd been stunned. We were here at the tomb—alone?

I'd led the girls into the chamber, where more candles cast soft light on a large, flat rock on the right side of the tomb. The girls had said nothing as we'd huddled there together. Somehow I'd known this was the place.

The next morning, Thursday, we'd planned to visit the Temple Mount. I'd heard how beautiful it was to approach it from the east, hiking down from the Mount of Olives in the morning light. But Morgan had woken up during the night with an upset stomach and a strange dream about Mary and Joseph. So rather than hike, we'd taken a taxi to the Lion's Gate, where I'd noticed a Temple Mount entrance on my map.

As we'd walked through the gate toward Temple Mount security, someone had called out, "Are you Muslim?"

"No," I'd said, suddenly realizing that it was a Muslim-only entrance.

They'd motioned to continue on the road we were already on. "Keep walking up the Via Dolorosa, then take the next left."

The road had been cobbled and uphill, and Morgan had began to tug on my hand. Usually she didn't want me to carry her anymore. Like all twinkled-eyed daughters, she was growing out of her dad's arms. But she'd kept tugging.

"Sweetheart," I'd asked, "do you want me to carry you?"

With a nod she'd lifted her arms—my little girl again.

Resting her hand on my neck, she'd sipped from her water bottle as we trudged along together. In time we'd turned left, found the entrance meant for us, and spent two special hours on the Temple Mount. By the end Morgan had been rejuvenated and become her old self again. She'd poured her bottled water over Ally's head.

It hadn't been until the next afternoon, as I'd watched the girls giggling in the pool, that it had dawned on me. The street where I'd carried Morgan was the Via Dolorosa, the Way of the Cross. Intellectually I'd known it, but I hadn't been thinking about it at the time. I had been focused only on my little girl. As she'd leaned softly against me, my sole desire had been simply to hold her, to ease her burden. Somehow carrying her had felt lighter than not carrying her. It had helped me to understand the love of Christ for us.

On Friday evening we'd planned a return to the Temple Mount plaza. All my travel books had said how interesting it was to watch the Jewish people welcome "Shabbat" at sunset.

Fresh from our swim, we'd strolled back toward the Old City. As we'd got closer, we'd found ourselves joined, at a noticeably eager pace, by Jewish families, hand in hand, sharply dressed. We'd turned onto King David Street, where for the past few days shopkeepers had been yelling at us to buy something. But no longer. The marketplace had been silent. Everything had shut down in anticipation of Shabbat.

Drawing near the Temple Mount, I'd expected the same serenity and solitude we'd experienced there earlier—Orthodox men rocking back and forth in prayer at the Western Wall, also called the Wailing Wall. The tradition dated back to the period following Jerusalem's destruction, when once a year the Gentile authorities had allowed the Jews to return home and mourn their vanquished Temple. Standing before the old retaining wall, the only remnant of the Temple, the Jews had wailed at the loss of their holy place and their homeland. Most Jews had stayed off the Mount itself—they hadn't wanted to risk treading where the Holy of Holies might have been. They'd come only to the wall, and wept, and prayed. Even today, Jewish men—and in a separate area, Jewish women—press tightly to the wall: to pray, to worship, to remember. It is one of the most solemn scenes on the planet.

But on this night it wasn't only solemnity that greeted us. No, as the plaza came into full view, another emotion filled the evening air . . .

Joy!

Circles of Jewish teenage girls danced hand in hand, singing. Not far away stomped a spirited line of Jewish boys, their hands on each other's shoulders, their yarmulkes hanging on for dear life. Closer to the wall, hundreds of Jews of all ages gathered socially in close conversation: the women and men in their respective quarters. Laughter and tears, hugs and clasps. The whole place burst with emotion. I was stunned by the pulsating energy of the place. (To view our home video of this evening, go to www.youtube.com/watch?v=DIqPAuSisuU&feature=plcp.)

Every so often a Jewish man or woman would break from the socializing to approach the wall and pray. Some rolled up prayer cards—slipping them into the cracks of the wall—then returned to the community, walking backyard. Many of the worshippers didn't turn away from the wall all evening. Why would they want to? This wall once protected the Temple of the Lord!

Watching these modern-day children of Israel, I found myself marveling anew. *What an interesting people God chose to reveal Himself to,* I thought. *What an interesting way they dress and worship and act.* Then I remembered! God hadn't selected a people who dressed and worshipped and acted that way. They dressed and worshipped and acted this way *because* God had chosen them.

Suddenly I had the strangest sensation wash over me. *Familiarity.* Somehow I felt right at home. How could this be? I was at a place I'd never been before . . . with thousands of people I'd never seen before. No one had really made any effort to welcome my daughters and me. We weren't even *Jewish.* Instead, we were *Christian.* How could we feel right at home?

I looked around the plaza at other Christians standing there. They also seemed happy to be part of the evening—Jerusalem was special to them too. Still, by the looks on their faces, they appeared to feel somewhat out of place. Their expressions seemed to say: *What an interesting experience this is. It's a little like church on Sunday morning . . . except that it's not church, it's not Sunday, and it's not morning.*

That was true. It wasn't church, it wasn't Sunday, and it wasn't morning. Instead, it was Friday evening under the stars—as it was for the first humans. And that's why I felt at home—not because of the people or the place, but because of something that transcends both.

Because of *Shabbat*—the sign of the Jews—I suddenly had a much deeper understanding of my own Judeo-Christian faith community.

Chapter 3

Judeo-Christian

"Every teacher of the law who has become a disciple in the kingdom of heaven is like the owner of a house who brings out of his storeroom new treasures as well as old." —Jesus of Nazareth (Matt. 13:52).

In his book *Why the Jews Rejected Jesus* David Klinghoffer explores one of the most sensitive questions of all time—a question that has confounded Christians through the centuries: How could so many of Jesus' own people not accept His messiahship?

A Jew himself, Klinghoffer gives many reasons Jews refused to accept Jesus of Nazareth as messiah. But above all of them stands one: the Jews spurned Jesus because the religion that He founded, Christianity, rejected the Torah.

"Jews," writes Klinghoffer, "have always considered the meaning of their existence to be summarized in the event before the Mountain of God where they encamped, three months after leaving Egypt, to hear God's commandments. It was the moment of birth for the Jewish people. On that occasion, the Lord introduced himself to the people this way: 'You have seen what I did to Egypt, and that I have borne you on wings of eagles and brought you to Me. And now, if you hearken well to Me and observe My covenant, you shall be to Me a kingdom of priests and a holy nation' (Ex. 19:4, 5).

"The covenant—the commandments—was the reason God brought the Jews to meet Him. There is no other purpose to Jewish existence. There is no other purpose to *human* existence. The Jews have long believed that the universe remains in existence only because they accepted the Torah, which obligated them to be a 'kingdom of priests,' ministering to other peoples, teaching them about God. The commandments were simply the terms of this relationship with God that Israel now entered into.

"To abandon those commandments was to abandon the whole meaning of Jewish existence. To give them up, you had to have an awfully good reason. Jews who ceased to believe in God had a reason. But Christianity had none that was satisfying. Accepting Christ, as his message was preached by Paul, means abrogating the commandments. Beyond the one solitary verse that could be understood as God's promising a new covenant—Jeremiah 31:31, which we have seen that Christians misconstrued—the Hebrew Bible offers no escape clause from the Jewish mission. If God really intended the Jews to regard themselves as 'dead' (as Paul put it) to the Sinai covenant, surely He ought to have made this crystal clear, repeated and emphasized it over and over, in that part of scripture that, when Paul came along, the Jews already regarded as authoritative. . . . Everything else Christians might argue on behalf of Jesus the Messiah, all the other rhetorical points they lodge in their disputations and pamphlets and polemics and apologetics, falls away before this simple fact. No authentic Messiah would inspire a religion that ended up calling upon the Jews to reject the manifest meaning of Sinai" (pp. 214, 215).

Klinghoffer's question demands an answer: Why *would* a Jewish Messiah set aside the faith that was so important to His own people?

The answer is: He wouldn't and didn't.

New Treasures as Well as Old

Sixty miles north of the Jerusalem Temple, Jesus of Nazareth stood in a fishing boat and spoke a powerful one-sentence parable that would define the kind of follower He was looking for: "Therefore," he said, "every teacher of the law who has become a disciple in the kingdom of heaven is like the owner of a house who brings out of his storeroom new treasures as well as old" (Matt. 13:52).

The imagery in the parable is that of a Jewish teacher of the law—a scribe—who has been listening to Jesus teach. There were, in fact, scribes who followed Jesus around and stood at the water's edge listening to Him. A scribe devoted himself to the study and teaching of the Hebrew Scriptures. You might say he woke up thinking about Genesis and went to bed pondering Malachi. The life of a scribe centered on Scripture, and, to this point in history, his treasure house was filled with the *Hebrew* Scriptures only—what we call the Old Testament.

But in this parable something dramatic has happened. The scribe has begun to recognize that the Scriptures he treasures so dearly are being fulfilled in the person of Jesus. Deep into the night the scribe goes back and forth in his scrolls, discovering Yeshua to be the fulfillment of Hebrew Scripture: king, priest, Son of David, Messiah.

And so the scribe adds a second room to his house—one filled with new treasure. We call it the New Testament.

The message of this remarkable parable isn't one of either/or. Of either old treasures or new ones. And yet as we look at the faith communities throughout the world, we do find a sense of either/or. We see the devotion of our Jewish friends to the Torah, to the commandments, to the Sabbath—but we also glimpse their rejection of the Lord of the Sabbath. Or their ignorance of Him. Many Israelis today don't even know who Jesus of Nazareth was.

By the same token, we observe many Christians celebrating the faith of the New Testament in beautiful ways—but often downplaying the ancient faith, as though one replaced the other. But the new did not dislodge the old. Instead, one built on the other—fulfilled the other.

Why is it, asks Sandra L. Richter, associate professor of Old Testament at Asbury Theological Seminary and author of *The Epic of Eden*, that most Christians "struggle with the study of the Old Testament? Certainly they recognize that the Old Testament is Scripture, are intrigued by its stories, and realize that there must be some significance to the first two thirds of that leather-bound book they are lugging around. Yet if you talk to the typical layperson you will find that they have not been involved in any sort of intentional study of the Old Testament since . . . well, they can't remember when" (p. 16).

Indeed, if God had intended to begin a brand-new religion, it would have made much more sense to start it somewhere else—in Italy or Persia or India or Arabia, where other religions came into being. But Jesus was born in Judea and was dedicated in a Jewish temple. It was not a new faith— it was the same faith. Nor was it salvation by grace replacing salvation by works. It was *always* salvation by grace. God had saved the children of Israel by grace at the Red Sea before He'd asked them to obey at Sinai.

It's a popular myth that Jews ever believed that their obedience saved them, says Richard Elofer, a Jewish convert to Christianity and former president of the Seventh-day Adventist Church in Israel. "The Jewish people," Elofer told me in an interview, "don't believe in salvation by works. For the Jews, salvation has always been by faith. Thus when they enter the Seventh-day Adventist Church, they continue to believe in salvation by faith, but the faith is about Jesus. When they were in Judaism, the faith was just because they were Jews. But it is always by faith."

The Treasure House: All Scripture

The church Jesus built was founded on Scripture—all of Scripture.

When we enter into both testaments of Scripture, we will encounter both rooms of the treasure house. In this house, the new treasures aren't at odds with the old treasures, like mismatched furniture in someone's living room. The cross doesn't conflict with the ark of the covenant. The messages delivered by the angel Gabriel in Luke don't contradict those presented by Gabriel in Daniel. Nor do the mind-blowing supernatural end-time events of Revelation undermine the mind-blowing supernatural origins of Genesis.

"The Bible," writes Richter, "is the saga of Yahweh and Adam, the prodigal son and his ever gracious heavenly Father; humanity in their rebellion and God in His grace. This narrative begins with Eden and does not conclude until the New Jerusalem is firmly in place. It is all one story. And if you are a believer, it is all your story" (p. 15).

"Christians," adds Elofer, "have rejected the law and the Sabbath. Jews have rejected Jesus. To have the full truth, we need both of them."

We must have the new treasures as well as old ones. New Testament as well as Old. To be a true follower of Jesus Christ is to be a Judeo-Christian in the best sense of the word: celebrating our faith in Christ—and celebrating the ancient faith as well. This was the essence of my Seventh-day Adventist faith, and as I'd stood there Friday evening in Jerusalem, I'd never felt more excited about it.

Chapter 4

Finding Rest Again

I hadn't always felt so excited to be a Seventh-day Adventist. Several years earlier, when I first started teaching at Southern Adventist University, I'd blow out of town as fast as possible. I'd finish my classes and office tasks and, with angst in my soul, race out of Collegedale to our subdivision 15 minutes away. Being on a college campus wasn't the issue—I'd always enjoyed college students, both at Southern and at Union College, where I had previously taught. The issue was, suddenly, being in such a heavily Adventist setting. Like many others through the years, I'd unexpectedly entered a wilderness of grappling with my Adventist faith.

This was awkward.

Not only had I grown up in the Adventist Church, but straight out of college I'd worked at the Adventist world church headquarters as an editor of the *Adventist Review* magazine. Being Adventist was a major part of my identity. With such a background, it felt strange to find myself re-examining my own denomination. Still, it was more important to me to follow biblical truth—wherever it led.

The impetus for this difficult period was a large number of our friends and relatives who were leaving the Seventh-day Adventist Church because they'd come to believe that being an Adventist was incompatible with being what they called a "New Covenant Christian." At the same time, several high-profile Adventist pastors I'd respected had departed the church, putting forth the same argument.

Our friends made many points that I agreed with—such as the heavy focus many Adventists have placed on the trivial at the expense of the important: majoring in minors and minoring in majors. Issues such as diet and dress have taken way too much of our time and focus. I also agreed with the critique that, at times, Adventist leaders and members have placed the writings of its church founders, especially Ellen White, on too high a pedestal. That was a legitimate critique. There was only one measure of faith: the Holy Scriptures. If Scripture alone can't support our fundamental beliefs, then they should be thrown out.

I was also less than thrilled with the way certain church members represented the wider church. I didn't like the billboard evangelism or end-time hype. Since Adventists don't believe in eternal hellfire, some members try to use hell-on-earth as a scare tactic. Once, outside an Adventist-run grocery store, I saw a wild-eyed, white-bearded man warning whoever would listen—in this case, a young Asian man who didn't seem to know how to get away—about the end of the world. "September 11 was only the start!" the man said, his face turning crimson. "The next time it's going to be a bombshell!" To me, the incident represented the worst of Adventism, and it repelled me all the more.

I talked often with close Adventist friends I respected, expressing my questions and struggles. I had no truer friend during this period than Clifford Goldstein—Adventist writer and editor. Cliff called me at least once a week not to debate but just to see how I was doing.

Others were there for me as well. Chris Blake, author and teacher, had registered plenty of his own concerns with the Adventist Church through the years. "My approach," he said, "is not to let the bad guys win."

"The church has problems," agreed my Australian friend Gary Krause, director of Adventist Mission. "But what appeals to me about the Adventist Church is its focus on wholeness."

Once a month I had lunch with my former journalism professor, R. Lynn Sauls, who systematically worked through difficult questions with me—and on his own dime bought me several pertinent books to read.

It dawned on me that I had to decide who the church was. Was it Mr. Bombshell, or was it people like Cliff and Chris and Gary and Sauls? When I looked in general at who emerged as the leaders of the church—wonderfully balanced people such as my former boss at the *Adventist Review*, William Johnsson, and my respected university president, Gordon Bietz—I found hope returning. I decided it wasn't any more fair to evaluate my church by its weakest representatives than it would be to condemn the Baptist Church because of those members who scream "God hates you!" at American soldiers. Every community has extremist elements—you can't judge a community by them.

Finally, I looked into the bright eyes of the university students where I taught. Compared with the empty expressions I often saw on public university campuses, Southern's students were absolutely the kind of people I wanted to be part of. I realized that my eyes had once been bright too.

Unrest Over a Rest Day

There was another area, however, on which our former Adventist friends really zeroed in—the Sabbath. They said that the "Old Covenant" observance of the Sabbath was a shadow of things to come, that it had been fulfilled in Christ, and that we no longer needed to rest on Sabbath because we now rested in Christ. The issue, they said, wasn't the Sabbath being changed to Sunday. Acknowledging that no biblical support existed for the sacredness of the Sabbath being transferred to Sunday, they instead said that they now believed that Sabbath rest had been fulfilled by our salvation rest in Christ.

Such a claim startled and challenged me—the idea that the Sabbath somehow detracted from the cross of Christ. I knew that our salvation was in Christ alone. And I certainly didn't view resting and worshipping on Sabbath as contributing in any way to my salvation, no more than my daughters' obedience coaxes me into loving them. As with God's other commands, I regarded resting on Sabbath simply as part of the life of faith—like prayer or Bible study. How could resting from our labors—and letting others rest from theirs—be a threat to the cross?

I did agree that at times some members of our church have put way too much focus on the seventh-day Sabbath, as if we had invented it ourselves. Some Adventists seem to pray "Thank You for the Sabbath" more than they pray "Thank You for the cross."

Once I was visiting a Sabbath school class in another town, and the teacher posed this question: "Is it possible for someone who doesn't keep the Sabbath to be saved?"

Raising my hand, I said, "I think it's possible for someone who *does* keep the Sabbath to be saved."

The teacher paused as he processed my word choice. "Well," he said, "that's certainly a different take."

I probably shouldn't have said that, but I was frustrated by the attitude that Sabbath observance contributes to our salvation. I knew that it didn't. No more than prayer or Bible study or living with integrity or helping abused children. We're saved by the all-sufficient work of Christ alone.

Tragically, sometimes our church hasn't been clear on that. Not long ago my grandmother died, and apparently she died worried, just as she lived worried. That's a terrible state of mind to be in—the idea that we have to be good enough. None of us are *good enough*. "For it is by grace you have been saved, through faith—and this not from yourselves, it is the gift of God" (Eph. 2:8).

One of the reasons I was interested in the new questions my friends were asking was that I saw changes in them. Many of them showed a deeper hunger for the Word of God. Where before some of them seemed rather ambivalent toward Bible study and church in general, they now studied the Word with a voracious appetite. They were filled with praise for Christ in a way they hadn't experienced before.

Not all the changes were positive, however. Some of our friends began making poor choices—the new "freedom" they felt became the liberty to indulge in alcohol and other things, which wasn't very impressive to Cindy and me. I can remember going to a restaurant at which some of our former Adventist friends giddily ordered wine and shrimp. It seemed a little silly to me. I guess there must have been such a heavy burden of legalism on some of them that they just wanted to get as far away from it as possible.

Reexamining Sabbath

Whatever their individual lifestyle choices, I took our friends' new questions seriously and wanted to research the Sabbath again for myself—especially the specific texts they cited.

I was already familiar, of course, with the Scripture passages in support of the Sabbath. In Genesis 2 (long before God gave the commandments at Sinai) the Lord rested on the seventh day, blessed it, and made it holy. In Exodus 16 God told the Israelites not to gather manna on the Sabbath, and then in Exodus 20 He wrote with His own finger the commandment to rest on Sabbath. Years earlier I'd noted how the actual Sabbath commandment didn't mention worship per se—it focused on resting from our labors. Sometimes our church has inaccurately defined Sabbathkeeping as churchgoing. But the commandment itself was primarily about resting from our labors—and letting others do the same. What that meant was that the opposite of Sabbath-keeping wasn't Sundaykeeping. Rather it was refusing to rest—or let others rest. So to me, there was a moral component to the fourth commandment. If a boss forced employees to work seven days a week, wouldn't we consider that immoral?

What place, then, did worship have on Sabbath? An important one. The Torah called the Sabbath "a day of sacred assembly" (Lev. 23:3), and Jesus Himself modeled a Sabbath of both rest and worship. The fact that the Gospel accounts written many years after Jesus' resurrection still included so much material about His teaching and practice of Sabbath observance—including His statement that the Sabbath was made for humanity—was a strong argument in favor of the enduring nature of the Sabbath. As late as the fifth century a historian named Socrates Scholasticus wrote: "For although almost all the churches throughout the world celebrate the sacred mysteries on the sabbath of every week, yet the Christians of Alexandria and at Rome, on account of some ancient tradition, have ceased to do this." So 400 years later (a period longer than the life span of the United States), Christians were still observing the Sabbath, though some had abandoned the Sabbath to distance themselves from the Jews.

Notwithstanding all this support for the continuance of the Sabbath into the Christian Church, I wanted to reexamine those New Testament passages that, on the surface, seemed to present a challenge to Sabbath observance after the cross. The critics of Sabbathkeeping particularly cited four: Romans 14:1-6, Galatians 4:8-10, Colossians 2:13-17, and Hebrews 4:9 (though only Colossians and Hebrews use the actual word "Sabbath"). I wanted to study them for myself and see where the evidence pointed.

Romans 14:1-6

One passage that people used to challenge the Sabbath was Romans 14:1-6, which discusses both diet and days in the early church—which Paul terms "disputable matters." The apostle wrote Romans for both Jewish and Gentile Christians.

First, in verses 1 through 4 we find two categories of people: those who ate everything and those who lived only on vegetables. Apparently, some considered the person who ate everything (namely meat) as having strong faith, while the person who consumed just vegetables had weak faith. Some commentators interpret the references to food as meaning the Jewish dietary laws—that those who ate only vegetables were still observing such laws and were thus weak in faith, while those who ate meat were strong in faith. The problem with such an interpretation is that Jews didn't eat only vegetables. *They ate meat too.* The debate over eating meat didn't pertain to Jewish food laws. In fact, the word "unclean" used later in verse 14 didn't mean "impure," indicating a Jewish food law. Rather, it simply indicates "common."

So what kind of food controversies existed at this time? In multiple places in the New Testament, such as 1 Corinthians 10, we find the dilemma of whether early believers should partake of meat previously sacrificed to idols. Some believers felt uncomfortable with this and avoided meat, while others thought it was fine because they knew that idols had no affect on the meat. Paul counseled people to use their own judgment. That was likely the case here in Romans 14—the strong in faith were able to handle eating food sacrificed to idols, but others were more sensitive. It was simply a matter of personal conscience.

Verses 5 and 6 list two more categories of people: those who considered "one day more sacred than another" and those who regarded "every day alike." Many commentators interpreted the vague term "day" here to mean Jewish holy days, including the Sabbath, concluding that they no longer made any difference.

It was interesting, I noted, that here Paul devoted much less time to the topic of days than to food. Twenty-one verses discuss food, while less than two concern the issue of days. It seemed highly doubtful to me that the apostle would so casually dismiss something as important as the Sabbath. It appeared much more likely that the days mentioned here were probably related to food.

Indeed, I learned that the Romans believed that certain days were best for fasting. A document from this period recommended fasting on Wednesday and Friday rather than on Monday and Thursday. It is like the modern-day equivalent of when is the best time to have devotions—first thing in the morning or just anytime? Or whether to put up a Christmas tree—or to hide Easter eggs. On such inconsequential issues, Paul counseled, let each person be convinced in their own mind.

Galatians 4:8-11

The second passage that, on the surface, seemed to challenge Sabbath-keeping in the New Testament was Galatians 4:8-11. Paul directed the book of Galatians primarily to new Gentile Christians.

In my study I learned that one can understand the phrase "special days and months and seasons and years" in two different ways. One interpretation sees it as the pagan calendar that the Gentile Galatians, formerly pagans, used to follow. "How is it that you are *turning back* to those weak and miserable principles?" might have meant that the Galatians were still clutching on to pagan observances centered on elements in the cosmos.

The second interpretation of "special days and months and seasons and years" regards the Galatians as now feeling obligated to observe all the holy days of the Jewish calendar—as urged by the Judaizers who had infiltrated the church. Indeed, a major theme in Galatians was how to respond to those Jews urging circumcision and the Law on these new Gentile converts.

Whatever the correct interpretation of "days and months and seasons and years," I realized the most important thing to remember was that Galatians was a book about justification—about being saved. Galatians 5:4 says, "You who are trying to be justified by law have been alienated from Christ; you have fallen away from grace."

To this point in history, the Jews had believed that a person had to first become a Jew to be saved by God's grace. But Paul says no, that isn't true. A person doesn't have to initially become a Jew to be saved—we are saved through Christ. The apostle himself continued to observe the Sabbath and, for that matter, the Jewish feasts as well (see 1 Cor. 5:8). But, he says, we don't rely on these things for our salvation, which comes only through faith in Christ.

Colossians 2:13-17

The most challenging text for me about the continuance of the Sabbath was Colossians 2:16, 17: "So let no one judge you in food or in drink, or regarding a festival or a new moon or sabbaths, which are a shadow of things to come, but the substance is of Christ" (NKJV). Like Galatians, Colossians focused primarily on new Gentile Christians.

On the surface, the passage seemed to challenge the perpetuity of the Sabbath, grouping it with Jewish feasts and new moons—and terming them all as "shadows." I noted the apparent progression in verse 16 of (yearly) festivals, (monthly) new moons, and (weekly) sabbath days—and the label of shadows that seems to apply to them all. How did we Adventists handle this? Was the weekly Sabbath in play here? And if so, had it been relegated to "shadow" status?

Sometimes our church has responded to the verse by declaring, "Well, it *can't* be the weekly Sabbath here, because the weekly Sabbath wasn't a shadow of things to come—it was a memorial of creation." The problem with such an explanation was that it was circular—it ruled out the Sabbath based on our own understanding of the Sabbath. That wasn't good enough for me. If the New Testament declared the Sabbath to be a shadow, then we must be open to that.

One Adventist theologian, Ron du Preez, has made a much stronger case that "sabbath days" in this passage was, in fact, another term for festivals. Initially that seemed strange to me, because then the verse would essentially read "festivals, new moons, and festivals." But in his book *Judging the Sabbath: Discovering What Can't Be Found in Colossians 2:16*, du Preez cited what scholars call a chiastic structure that Hebrew writers often used. A chiasm is when you start with something, then move to something else, then return to the first thing—a pattern we can diagram as ABBA. For example, the Gospel of John opens with a chiastic structure:

In the beginning was the Word, (A)
and the Word was with God, (B)
and the Word was God. (B)
He was in the beginning with God. (A)

Du Preez pointed to Hosea 2:11, which says, "I will stop all her celebrations: her yearly festivals, her New Moons, her Sabbath days—all her appointed festivals." The passage speaks of both festivals and Sabbath days as appointed feasts. The weekly Sabbath wasn't an appointed feast, so the term "Sabbath days" in this sequence must refer to some of the annual festivals. Maybe that's what was going on in Colossians 2, where we find the exact same wording.

But suppose that the weekly Sabbath *was* in view in Colossians 2. Did that mean it had been fulfilled along with the feasts and new moons? Not necessarily. Here's why: Whenever we find the sequence of feasts, new moons, and sabbaths in the Old Testament, it's almost always within one particular context: *sacrifices.* Ezekiel 45:17, for example, states: "And it shall be the prince's part to give burnt offerings, and meat offerings, and drink offerings, in the feasts, and in the new moons, and in the sabbaths, in all solemnities of the house of Israel" (KJV). I noticed how the Ezekiel passage used similar terms as Colossians 2: meat, drink, feasts, new moons, sabbaths. The clear context was instructions for *sacrifices.*

So what could Paul mean by "shadows" in Colossians 2:16? Most scholars argue that the shadows are the feasts, new moons, and sabbaths. The problem with that approach, I discovered, was that a new moon couldn't be a "shadow," because a new moon had no religious significance in itself—only its association with *sacrifices.* Instead, I realized the shadows must have something to do with what all these particular days had in common: the sacrifices *offered* on them.

Indeed, at this time many Jewish Christians were still offering sacrifices and making judgments about Christians who didn't. Paul himself experienced this in Acts 21 when he went back to Jerusalem and found himself pressured to participate in a purification rite, which included sacrifices.

Was it possible, I wondered, that the missing piece to the puzzle here was "sacrifices"—that that's what this passage was talking about? Was there scriptural support for the idea that "shadow" in Colossians 2 referred to sacrifices, even though it doesn't specifically mention them?

Yes, there was. Strong support. I discovered that the only two other New Testament references to "shadows" were associated with sacrifices. They appear in Hebrews, a book likely written or influenced by Paul. Hebrews 8:3, 5: "Every high priest is appointed to offer both gifts and sacrifices. . . . They serve at a sanctuary that is a copy and shadow of what is in heaven." Hebrews 10:1, 5: "The law is only a shadow of the good things that are coming—not the realities themselves. For this reason it can never, by the same sacrifices repeated endlessly year after year, make perfect those who draw near to worship. . . . Therefore, when Christ came into the world, he said: 'Sacrifice and offering you did not desire, but a body you prepared for me.'"

Each passage links the terms "shadow" with "sacrifices." I began to see a clear theme here: the sacrifices were the shadows, while the body of Christ was the substance. Both Colossians and Hebrews taught that the age of sacrifices was now over. They were shadows of something better to come: the body of Christ.

Hebrews 4:9

There was one other reference to "Sabbath"—one that came with great peace and gentleness: "There remains, then, a Sabbath-rest for the people of God" (Heb. 4:9).

It too has sometimes been misunderstood. Some Adventists have said that the writer of Hebrews was arguing that the Sabbath day still remains—as though there were controversy about it. But actually, the author didn't use the typical word for Sabbath here, but instead a unique term, *sabbatismos*, which means a "Sabbath-like rest."

He wasn't saying here that the Sabbath remains for the people of God, but rather that a Sabbath-like rest remains for the people of God. It was our salvation rest—resting in God. The writer compared our salvation rest to our Sabbath rest. If the Sabbath were no longer in existence, why would the biblical author have used the term *sabbatismos,* Sabbath-like rest? Rather than being defensive or strained, he used the familiar term *Sabbath* to explain God's rest. This promise of resting in God *remained* from the time of Israel's entrance into the Promised Land.

Suddenly a lightbulb went on in my head, and I realized what this meant: both God's rest and Sabbath rest coexisted in the Old Covenant—and both continue to exist in the New Covenant. The Sabbath rest and God's salvation rest both endure through faith in Jesus Christ.

Written on Our Hearts

So what really happened to the seventh-day Sabbath? Why do most Christians no longer practice it? The simple but uncomfortable answer is that Christians began to distance themselves from the Sabbath in order to distinguish themselves from the Jews. Many early Christian documents reflect animosity toward the Jews and the Jewish Sabbath. Canon 29 from the Council of Laodicea (A.D. 364) reads: "Christians must not judaize by resting on the Sabbath, but must work on that day, rather honouring the Lord's Day (Sunday); and, if they can, resting then as Christians. But if any shall be found to be judaizers, let them be anathema from Christ."

It certainly wouldn't be fair to say that Christians today distance themselves from the Sabbath because they do not want to be confused with Jews. It's simply a situation that Christians have, in many cases, unknowingly inherited from another time and place. I have no doubt that as more and more Christians trace their Jewish roots, they will come to view the Sabbath through new eyes.

An Adventist friend of mine, Geoff, was working as a new community organizing resident in San Francisco through Jewish Funds for Justice. At a weekend retreat Geoff met his roommate, Rabbi Adams.

"What's your faith tradition?" the rabbi asked.

"Seventh-day Adventist," Geoff replied, wondering what to expect.

The rabbi raised his eyebrows. "May I ask you a question?"

"Sure," Geoff said.

The rabbi leaned forward. "Why aren't all Christians Adventists? I mean, how do people breathe without the Sabbath?"

With all of our faults—and we have many—one of the most beautiful things about the Seventh-day Adventist Church is that we celebrate salvation in Christ alone as taught in the New Testament—and we also celebrate our Jewish heritage found in the timeless commandments written by the finger of God. This is the new covenant: the words of God written not just on stone and given to one people, but written on the hearts of all. Adventists have been entrusted with a special responsibility: bringing forth treasures new and old. (Indeed, more Seventh-day Adventists now keep the Sabbath than any other group in the world, including Jews.) From our very beginnings, our church has called people to the fullness of God's treasure house: to "obey God's commandments and remain faithful to Jesus" (Rev. 14:12).

When the Family Splits

Through the years Cindy and I have met other Adventists who have entered the desert of grappling with their faith. Some, like us, were challenged by friends, family members, and people they respected. Others realized that they'd never really studied out their faith for themselves. When I hear about people who have developed a deeper love for Christ and His Word, I don't feel too troubled. It is better to know Christ outside the Adventist Church than not to know Him inside of it.

What does disturb me is those who leave the church casting aspersions on Adventist friends and family members they've left behind—as though Adventists can't possibly know and love the same Jesus and the same Scriptures as much as they do. In behaving that way, former Adventists exhibit the same negative traits they found so repugnant in the first place—they've simply moved their chairs to the other side of the table. To those who have left, I would say: Don't let your identity be a "former" anything. Let your focus be on Christ, and be Christlike and loving toward all, including your Adventist family and friends.

Rest for Your Soul

After about three years of grappling and reexamination, Cindy and I began to find rest again in our Adventist faith. One Sunday morning my family and I drove out to the country. For several months Sunday morning had been a time we'd been visiting other Christian churches to see what was out there. We truly enjoyed our fellowship with other Christian believers we met, and we found a great deal to admire in their faith communities—including a warm spirit of acceptance and a strong male presence in church ministry. We also found some things that disappointed us, including poor lifestyle choices and surprising unfamiliarity with Scripture. Ultimately, we realized that the grass at home was a lot greener than some of our friends were saying.

As we drove that morning through the hills and valleys of Tennessee, our daughter Ally said, "What are we doing, Daddy?"

"Healing," I said.

Cindy sighed and nodded. We both had some healing to do.

If you're in the desert now, talk to those who have been there. They will help you find rest for your soul.

Chapter 5

Jesus of Nazareth: The Treasure of Heaven

I wonder whether there may have been, wandering among the hundreds of thousands of Jews arriving in Jerusalem the Passover week that Jesus died, a little Jewish girl playing just outside the east gate of the city near the Mount of Olives—a little Jewish girl who happened to brush up against a small stray donkey and, as she did, wondered to herself: *Why does that little donkey smell like perfume?*

The perfume that would have emanated from the animal—a donkey's colt, actually—would not have been like those we smell today. The fragrance wasn't necessarily sweet as we know it. It was more earthy, more warm and musky. But it would have been very special to that little Jewish girl—to all Jewish people. Because those who had ever had the privilege of smelling pure nard, who knew anything about it, would recognize just how precious it was.

Nard, or spikenard oil, came from the spikenard herb that grew in what we know today as the Himalayan mountains of India. Jewish people, perhaps blushing a little, would have read sensual descriptions of nard perfume in the Song of Solomon 1:12—"While the king *is* at his table, my spikenard sends forth its fragrance" (NKJV). To have even a small cup of nard would have been considered a great luxury. A whole pound or pint of nard would cost the equivalent of perhaps $20,000 today.

And that's why it would have been so curious that a donkey's colt would have smelled like nard. It wouldn't have made any sense. To a Jew, the only possible reference point for a colt bearing traces of an extravagant perfume would be found in 1 Kings 1, which described how the newly anointed King Solomon, the son of King David, was drenched in regal perfumes and rode into Jerusalem, where the people shouted, "Long live King Solomon, save now King Solomon." Or put another way: "Hosanna to the son of David."

It was the only time a colt would have had the scent of perfume—the entrance of the king of Israel himself, covered in fragrance so heavily that it would have spread even to the animal the king was riding on. But Israel hadn't had a real king in a very long time. So why would this particular colt, at this particular time, smell like perfume? What on earth was going on?

"Then Mary took about a pint of pure nard, an expensive perfume; she poured it on Jesus' feet and wiped his feet with her hair. And the house was filled with the fragrance of the perfume" (John 12:3).

In a Jewish home, washing the feet of a guest or anointing a guest with oil was a commonly expected act of hospitality. What was unusual is how far Mary went. First, she let her hair down in public, something not considered appropriate. Only prostitutes typically did that. Then she poured a whole pint of valuable perfume on the feet of Jesus. No one in Israel ever used that amount of perfume unless they were doing one of two things: anointing a king or priest, or anointing a body for burial.

The Hebrew word for "messiah" is pronounced *mashiach*, which means "the anointed one." The word alludes to the ceremony used to set apart someone chosen by God, such as a king or a priest. "Instead of being crowned during a coronation," writes Ann Spangler and Lois Tverberg in *Sitting at the Feet of Rabbi Jesus,* "Hebrew kings were anointed with sacred oil perfumed with extremely expensive spices. Only used for consecrating objects in the temple and for anointing priests and kings, this sacred anointing oil would have been more valuable than diamonds. The marvelous scent that it left behind acted like an invisible 'crown,' conferring an aura of holiness on its recipients. Everything and everyone with that unique fragrance was recognized as belonging to God in a special way.

"In the ancient Middle East, the majesty of a king was expressed not only by what he wore—his jewelry and robes—but by his royal 'aroma.' Even after a king was first anointed, he would perfume his robes with precious oils for special occasions. . . . During royal processions, the fragrance of expensive oils would inform the crowds that a king was passing by" (pp. 16, 17).

Only a newly anointed king or priest would get the kind of perfume drenching that Jesus received here. The fragrance would have lingered on Him throughout the final week of His life—at the last supper; in Gethsemane; as He was arrested; as He was questioned, spit on, and beaten; and as He was mocked, whipped, stripped naked, crucified, and placed in a tomb. Throughout all of it, people would not be able to escape the fragrance of royalty that emanated from Him.

"The next day the great crowd that had come for the festival heard that Jesus was on his way to Jerusalem. They took palm branches and went out to meet him, shouting, 'Hosanna!' 'Blessed is he who comes in the name of the Lord!' 'Blessed is the king of Israel!'

"Jesus found a young donkey and sat upon it, as it is written, 'Do not be afraid, Daughter of Zion; see, your king is coming, seated on a donkey's colt'" (verses 12-15).

Until this point in His life Jesus had been somewhat guarded about who He was—about what He allowed people to say about Him. Those days were now over. No longer would He state that His time had not yet come—it was now here. And no longer would He hold anything back. Drenched in perfume, He rode into Jerusalem, His feet dangling against the donkey's sides. The Jewish people viewed the creatures as noble animals. A king rode a horse during war, but he rode a donkey during peacetime.

"Many people . . . went out to meet him. So the Pharisees said to one another, 'See, this is getting us nowhere. Look how the whole world has gone after him!'

"Now there were some Greeks among those who went up to worship at the festival. They came to Philip, who was from Bethsaida in Galilee, with a request. 'Sir' they said, 'we would like to see Jesus.' Philip went to tell Andrew; Andrew and Philip in turn told Jesus.

"Jesus replied, 'The hour has come for the Son of Man to be glorified. . . . Now my soul is troubled, and what shall I say? "Father, save me from this hour"? No, it was for this very reason I came to this hour. Father, glorify your name!'" (verses 18-28).

Thousands of years earlier God had promised Abraham that someday his people would bless all the people of the earth. That promise was now being fulfilled. A descendant of Abraham, Jesus knew the significance of Gentiles asking for an audience with Him. The dividing walls were breaking down.

The Greek believers were among thousands of foreigners who journeyed to Jerusalem to worship at the Feast of Passover. Seven weeks later, at the Feast of Pentecost, both Jews and Greeks from every nation would be stunned to hear Jesus' disciples preaching in the language of their own land. The message was crystal clear: all people of the earth were to now receive the blessings of Israel.

"Jesus knew that the Father had put all things under his power, and that he had come from God and was returning to God; so he got up from the meal,

took off his outer clothing, and wrapped a towel around his waist. After that, he poured water into a basin and began to wash his disciples' feet, drying them with the towel that was wrapped around him" (John 13:3-5).

When Jesus unexpectedly rose from the Passover table and began washing His disciples' feet, He was doing much more than demonstrating servant leadership. He was preparing His priests for ministry. "You do not realize now what I am doing," He hinted to a perplexed Peter, "but later you will understand" (verse 7).

In the Old Covenant sanctuary system the priests could not enter the tabernacle until they had first washed their feet and hands in a basin just outside the tabernacle curtain: "Then the Lord said to Moses, 'Make a bronze basin, with its bronze stand, for washing. Place it between the tent of meeting and the altar, and put water in it. Aaron and his sons are to wash their hands and feet with water from it. Whenever they enter the tent of meeting, they shall wash with water so that they will not die'" (Ex. 30:17-20).

This was what Jesus was doing with His disciples—His New Covenant priests. He was symbolically cleansing their feet in a basin. What about their hands? As part of the Passover meal, the disciples would have already cleansed their hands—but not their feet. A towel wrapped around His waist, Christ our High Priest cleansed the disciples' feet, symbolically transferring their dirt onto Himself. He was literally wrapped in our sins. Years later Peter would write: "'He himself bore our sins' in his body on the cross, so that we might die to sins and live for righteousness; 'by his wounds you have been healed'" (1 Peter 2:24). "But you are a chosen people, a royal priesthood, a holy nation, God's special possession, that you may declare the praises of him who called you out of darkness into his wonderful light" (verse 9).

"When he had finished praying, Jesus left with his disciples and crossed the Kidron Valley. On the other side there was a garden, and he and his disciples went into it" (John 18:1).

During Passover week the priests sacrificed thousands and thousands of lambs at the Temple just up the hill from the Kidron Valley. The blood from the lambs poured onto the altar, then flowed down a channel to a brook that ran through the Kidron Valley. The brook may have turned red from the blood of the lambs. Jesus and His disciples would have crossed over the red waters of the brook on their way to Gethsemane.

"Now Judas, who betrayed him, knew the place, because Jesus had

often met there with his disciples. So Judas came to the garden, guiding a detachment of soldiers and some officials from the chief priests and Pharisees. They were carrying torches, lanterns and weapons.

"Jesus, knowing all that was going to happen to him, went out and asked them, 'Who is it you want?'

"'Jesus of Nazareth,' they replied.

"'I am he,' Jesus said. . . . When Jesus said 'I am he,' they drew back and fell to the ground" (verses 2-6).

Only Jesus actually used the words "I Am." "I Am" is the meaning of the Old Testament name of Yahweh. When Jesus was walking on the water and the disciples were terrified, Jesus called out: "I Am. Don't be afraid." In other words: "Yahweh. Don't be afraid."

"Jesus answered, 'I told you that I am he. If you are looking for me, then let these men go'" (verse 7).

By the time Jesus emerged from Gethsemane, He had the look of a parent absolutely determined to save His lost children. He was absolutely dead set on completing His mission, because He was absolutely in love with the people on our planet. There *was* no stopping Him.

"Then Pilate took Jesus and had him flogged. The soldiers twisted together a crown of thorns and put it on his head. They clothed him in a purple robe and went up to him again and again, saying, 'Hail, king of the Jews!' And they struck him the face. . . .

"'Here is your king,' Pilate said to the Jews.

"But they shouted, 'Take him away! Take him away! Crucify him!'

"'Shall I crucify your king?' Pilate asked.

"'We have no king but Caesar,' the chief priests answered" (John 19:1-15).

Flogging was to have your back ripped open. The whips the soldiers used were embedded with small, jagged rocks, which tore the flesh. Many prisoners didn't survive it. To have a crown of thorns driven into your head and to be jeered at by your own people—who then declare that they have no king but Caesar—would have been a sickening experience: the Hebrew people, the ones led to Jerusalem by the Lord Himself, now declaring that they have no king but Caesar? But not for a moment did Jesus hesitate or attempt to spare His own life. Instead, the resolved Messiah led the multitude up the road to the fulfillment of a covenant that says the penalty for sin must be death.

Carrying his own cross, he went out to the place of the Skull (which in Aramaic is called Golgotha). There they crucified him, and with him two others—one on each side and Jesus in the middle" (John 19:17, 18).

The middle was the place reserved for the worst criminal. It was supposed to be the position of Barabbas—a murderer. The criminals on either side were likely associates of Barabbas. Barabbas was not a first name but a last name. Bar means "son of," just as Simon bar Jonah meant "son of Jonah" or Bartholomew meant "son of lomew." (Bartholomew was probably the last name of the disciple Nathanael.): Barabbas meant "son of abbas"— meaning "son of the father." Many early manuscripts record Barabbas's first name as Yeshua (Jesus). Yeshua was a common name at the time meaning "Yahweh saves." So Barabbas' name was along the lines of "Yahweh saves, son of the father."

Here the true Son of the Father takes Barabbas' place—cursed and hanging on a tree. The Son of God has become the Son of Man, a new Adam naked before God on a Friday morning.

"*When the soldiers crucified Jesus, they took his clothes, dividing them into four shares, one for each of them, with the undergarment remaining. This garment was seamless, woven in one piece from top to bottom.*

"*'Let's not tear it,' they said to one another. 'Let's decide by lot who will get it'*" (verses 23, 24).

A Jewish man would typically wear five items of clothing: shoes, turban, girdle, tunic, and outer robe. Jesus' tunic was "woven in one piece from top to bottom."

Many Jews expected two messiahs: a kingly messiah and a priestly one. Both the king figure and the priest figure were very important each in themselves, and the Jews didn't see how the messiah could be summed up in one person. The kingly messiah, as prophesied, would come from the tribe of Judah, from Bethlehem. The priestly messiah would presumably emerge from the priestly tribe of Levi. That's why the Jews were so interested in John the Baptist. Since John was from the tribe of Levi, they wondered if he might be the priestly messiah. The Jews had no inkling that one individual could be both king and priest, even though Zechariah had strangely prophesied about a "priest on his throne" (Zech. 6:13).

Exodus 28:31, 32 described the attire of a priest: "Make the robe . . . entirely of blue cloth, with an opening for the head in its center. There shall be a woven edge like a collar around this opening, so that it will not tear." The priest dressed in a robe woven in one piece from top to bottom—the type that Jesus wore to the cross.

Jesus wasn't from the priestly line of Levi, but rather from an earlier, more mysterious lineage. The book of Hebrews explained that Christ belonged to the priestly order of Melchizedek, a priest "without father or mother, without genealogy" (Heb. 7:3) to whom Abraham himself once paid a tithe. Melchizedek also happened to be the king of a little town called Salem—a place later known as Jerusalem.

A king from the line of Judah and a priest from that of Melchizedek—all wrapped up in one messiah. Who's in complete control here? The only thing as structured and systematic as the giving of the old covenant was the fulfillment of that same covenant at the cross of Calvary. On this very afternoon, at the moment of Jesus' death, the Temple curtain from the old covenant will be torn from top to bottom, ushering in a new covenant presided over by a new high priest, Jesus Christ. No longer would a veil separate us from the presence of the Father. "Therefore, brothers and sisters, since we have confidence to enter the Most Holy Place by the blood of Jesus, by a new and living way opened for us through the curtain, that is, his body" (Heb. 10:20).

"Later, knowing that everything had now been finished, and so that the Scripture would be fulfilled, Jesus said, 'I am thirsty.' A jar of wine vinegar was there, so they soaked a sponge in it, put the sponge on a stalk of the hyssop plant, and lifted it to Jesus' lips. When he had received the drink, Jesus said, 'It is finished.' With that, he bowed his head and gave up his spirit" (John 19:28-30).

The wine vinegar that Jesus received here isn't to be confused with the wine mixed with gall that the Gospel of Matthew described as being offered to Jesus earlier in the day. Just before Jesus was crucified, about 9:00 in the morning, the soldiers had offered Jesus wine and gall. Gall, a bitter-tasting poison, would have deadened the pain. Jesus refused the vinegar mixed with gall.

Six hours later—3:00 in the afternoon—Jesus accepted the wine vinegar raised to Him on the stalk of a hyssop plant. His focus here wasn't His suffering but fulfilling Scripture. It was Passover evening. Thousands of years earlier, as the Hebrews were leaving Egypt, they smeared the blood of a lamb on the doorposts of their homes as protection against the angel of death who passed over. The instruction was to "take a bunch of hyssop, dip it into the blood in the basin and put some of the blood on the top and on both sides of the doorframe. . . . When the Lord goes through the land . . . he will see the blood on the top and sides of the doorframe and will pass over that doorway, and he will not permit the destroyer to enter your houses and strike you down" (Ex. 12:22, 23). Jesus is not only king and priest, but also the lamb of God that covers the sins of the world.

The Lord gave one additional instruction about the Passover lamb: its bones must not be broken.

"*Now it was the day of Preparation, and the next day was to be a special Sabbath. Because the Jewish leaders did not want the bodies left on the crosses during the Sabbath, they asked Pilate to have the legs broken and the bodies taken down. The soldiers therefore came and broke the legs of the first man who had been crucified with Jesus, and then those of the other. But when they came to Jesus and found that he was already dead, they did not break his legs. Instead, one of the soldiers pierced Jesus' side with a spear, brining a sudden flow of blood and water*" (John 19:31-34).

Since Jesus had already died, the soldiers did not break His legs to make breathing difficult and hasten death. But just to make sure, a soldier thrust a spear into Jesus' side, bringing forth blood and water that flowed down onto his sin-covered waist and his perfume-covered feet.

"*These things happened so that the scripture would be fulfilled: 'Not one of his bones will be broken' and . . . 'They will look on the one they have pierced'*" (verses 36, 37).

Part 2

Being the
Adventist Church

Chapter 6

One Sabbath Morning

One morning in my university classroom I noticed that several of my journalism students were especially dragging. "OK," I said, "what's going on? I can tell you're thinking about something—but I doubt it's this class." They laughed.

"Honestly, what did you wake up thinking about today?" I asked.

For the next 10 minutes the stories and prayer requests poured in: stressful schedules, parents without work, a dying grandmother, a friend in a bad relationship.

The many burdens those students quietly carried now deeply moved me. Who can truly know what's on the minds of the people around us? (A colleague of mine includes this tag on every e-mail she sends: "Be kinder than necessary, because everyone you meet is fighting some kind of battle.")

My students and I got to talking about how the local church was like our classroom. Each Sabbath morning people from all kinds of situations—with all kinds of burdens—come together in one setting. But behind the smiles and courtesies, what's *really* on their minds? As an impromptu assignment, I invited my students to show up at my local church the following Sabbath morning and interview the people arriving. With their names changed, here's what the church members had to say:

Dawn: Praying for Wisdom

Dawn has tired eyes. When she woke up this morning to get ready for church, she was so exhausted she couldn't think. Having two sons, ages 7 and 10, and a full-time job will do that.

Yet, what tires her the most also brings her the most joy. She sits at church with her family, leaning toward her husband, her right hand gently rubbing her oldest son's back. Though she jokes that sometimes she feels ready to kill them, she says life would be empty without them. "I wouldn't have it any other way," she says with a smile.

Because of that, Dawn prays for wisdom in raising two boys—that God will lead her to do the right thing in dealing with her kids. During the sermon her youngest son takes her hand.

After a busy week, she has come to church to be renewed with Christ, and after only a few minutes, she looks less tired and more at ease than when she came in. Church is her haven, but she doesn't worship selfishly, retreating inside herself. She is conscious of her family as they worship together. When the service is over, she looks recharged, ready for anything the coming week might bring. As she gets up from her seat, Dawn's eyes look brighter.

—By Raquel Levy

Brad: Seemingly Flawless

Maybe it's his age, a college student in his 20s, or maybe it's his perfectly messy blond hair that portrays such confidence. Either way, Brad has his act together. His neatly pressed blue-and-white-striped button-down shirt and khaki pants complete his poised look. From the outside, it's as if he has nothing to hide.

As a double major in nursing and music, Brad prays about schoolwork more than anything else. His majors reveal that he isn't afraid of a challenge—the grand endeavor of intertwining the hope of financial stability with what makes him happy. Despite his ambition, he has a downfall: procrastination. That is where praying comes in most.

But prayers about school are not the only aspect of Brad's spiritual pursuit. He fondly remembers a special Friday night church service that really touched him and enhanced his walk with God. Plus, the Christian music, the fellowship with friends, and the sense of community he finds at church keep him returning week after week.

Amid his busy lifestyle, Brad's deepest desire and greatest challenge is to open the Bible and read it every day. "I have aspirations like the rest of the world," he says, "but before I can be something, I have to be right with God."

—By Amy Vitrano

LeAnn: Joyful Anyway

LeAnn is a greeter at church. Today she's wearing a flared skirt, blue tights, and tall, black boots. Her hair is long, her eyes are green and bright, and she is smiling. She's in her 20s, recently married. Every person LeAnn greets at the door receives a "Happy Sabbath" that is so genuine, others can't help smiling back.

As happy as she is, a heavy burden weighs on her heart. A friend has brain cancer. She has had surgery, but the tumor keeps coming back. It worries LeAnn even more since her own father died of cancer.

LeAnn is joyful despite the concerns she carries. When asked what brings her so much joy, she bubbles with answers: nature, watching the clouds, being married, and church. "I love church. I miss it when I'm not here," she said. "For me, church is a place to come and be open and raw with God."

When the service starts, LeAnn waits a few minutes at the back of the sanctuary to make sure no latecomer goes ungreeted. Then, after scanning the seats for her husband, she goes to sit with him. During the service she cuddles under his arm and listens.

When the final song concludes, she finds those she missed earlier and greets them with a hug and a smile. Then she and her husband make their way out.

—By Ashley Wagner

Eric: Serious About His Mornings

A teenager walks down the center aisle as he looks for a place to sit. He seems focused and serious.

Eric confesses that he is here today because he wants to eat lunch. His parents are going to a friend's home after the service for dinner, and he didn't want to miss it by staying home. But this high school junior with sandy-blond hair insists that not every Sabbath is this way.

"I like church, and I don't view it as a bother," he explains, realizing that what he said first could be taken the wrong way.

During the week Eric wakes up around 5:45 a.m., prepares breakfast for himself, makes his mom coffee, and then sits down to read the paper before heading off to school.

He says that his grades are what bring him the most satisfaction. "I have all A's and one B, but it's a 92 so it will be an A soon," he comments nonchalantly. "I like doing well in school and being smart."

Although Eric is already thinking about what he will study in college, he hasn't settled on a major yet. He says he likes research, history, and science and is trying to decide between becoming either a lawyer or doctor.

—By Suzanne Ocsai

Sandy: Looking Out for Others

A young woman sits in the back of the auditorium and waits patiently for church to begin. She anticipates her opportunity to go up front and lead the song service. That's what she woke up thinking about this morning—leading others in praising God.

The heaviest thing on Sandy's heart is whether or not those around her are prepared for heaven. Are the people in her life ready for Jesus to return? She prays to God about this more than anything else—it's been on her mind a lot lately.

As she leads worship, she stands in front of the microphone and closes her eyes. The congregation can see her soaking in His love and praising Him through her music as she sways to each song. During the sermon she sits beside the pastor's wife in the front row, listening quietly but diligently.

As she returns to the stage for the closing song, she lifts her hands toward heaven. It's the little things that she enjoys most in life—the small joys or bits of humor that God tosses into each day.

—By Jaime Jacobson

Mike and Jill: Kid-centered Lives

Mike and Jill are in their 30s and parents of two toddlers. During the sermon Mike takes their 4-year-old daughter to get a drink of water, while Jill goes outside the sanctuary so that their son can burn off some energy.

The 2-year-old boy laughs and wobbles down the hall as his mother chases after him. She appears tired and stressed but makes sure her son doesn't leave her sight. Family matters fill her mind. She says she wants to raise her kids to be good people, but with her husband Mike working and pursuing a master's degree, they don't find as much time for spiritual things during the week as they would like.

"I knew having kids and a family was a commitment," Mike observes. "When I was younger, I had more time for myself."

Mike and Jill say it's their kids who keep them going to church. "My kids love it," says Jill, who is now holding their son. "They expect to see their friends and go to Sabbath school. We haven't been to church the past few weeks, because this one won't sit still."

She pauses midthought to tell her son that if he doesn't stop moving around, she will spank him. He doesn't. She does.

Shortly afterward, Mike and his daughter meet up with his wife and son. They leave church early.

—By Kevin Gutierrez

Yvonne: Alone

Yvonne walks through the door alone. Dressed in a conservative long, gray dress and a blue scarf, she appears to be in her 20s. When she woke up this morning, her first thought was how happy she was to get to church early because she had missed attending the week before. In her prayer life she focuses especially on her family, friends, and herself.

She has lived most of her life alone. Yvonne was forced to grow up quickly when she went to England alone for high school at age 17, and since returning to the U.S. after college, she has lived by herself. As a result she has become a woman who thinks for herself and has stopped relying on her parents.

Her parents' unstable relationship is the main reason that Yvonne has remained single. She is afraid of marriage. Yet despite her fears, Yvonne says she lives a happy life and doesn't blame God for her situation.

—By Brenda Adeleke

Together

How much we all have on our minds—and how tender we should be with those around us.

Jesus knew the living hell of a hurting body. The divisions among us can cause great strife and pain. Pastor Jim Cymbala writes that the greatest threat to the church isn't crack cocaine or financial pressures—it's the body destroying itself through harsh words. If there's anything we can do 100 percent of the time, it's to find fault in the people around us. Every one of us is an easy target for criticism. We must choose to be patient with each other. Unfortunately, we tend to be much more patient with ourselves than we do with others.

A church in which members look for the good in each other and encourage each other is a tremendously healthy church—and can do great things for Christ.

A Matter of Perspective

Often the key to togetherness is the vantage point we choose to take—whether our focus is on petty details or the big picture.

In the small Minnesotan town in which I grew up, I went primarily to public school. Whenever our school had a big game against another nearby town, we didn't like that town. They were our enemy, at least for the two-hour game. We hated Wadena and we hated Fergus Falls and we especially hated Staples. If there was a basketball game against Staples, we didn't like the people of Staples. (What kind of name was Staples, anyway?) As one Minnesotan town played against another Minnesotan town, those towns were enemies.

But what about when our whole state of Minnesota played against another state? Consider our baseball team—the Minnesota Twins. What about when they went against the dreaded New York Yankees? Then we weren't enemies with other Minnesotan towns. We were friends—brothers and sisters, fellow Minnesotans—and together we booed New York.

Suppose all our states were on the same side, as in the Olympics. Well, then we loved the other states. Wisconsin and Michigan and Illinois were our friends, our brothers and sisters. And together we disliked Russia.

The higher we lift our sights, the more the differences don't matter. It's not that they disappear, but rather that they aren't our focus anymore, because we're focused on something bigger. A lot of people don't care for New York, but on the evening of September 11, 2001, we all became New Yorkers.

Once a church I visited had a time of prayer at the close of the service. A young man slipped out from his seat and fell down in prayer in the aisle. Immediately a half dozen of his friends, from wherever they were seated, rushed to the aisle and knelt in prayer with him. When one part of the body was hurting, they were all hurting. They were together—they were one.

Chapter 7

Listening to Each Other

Let's say that one spring you and three of your friends decide to take a road trip up the East Coast to Washington, D.C., and New York City. You spend about a week traveling, and when you return, the four of you get together with a wider group of your friends to talk about your adventures.

Someone asks, "How was Washington, D.C.?" And your friends reply, "Oh, it was great." And they talk about how peaceful it was at the Lincoln Memorial and how pretty the cherry blossoms were at the National Mall. With excitement they tell about seeing the president's motorcade rushing past one afternoon.

And you say, "Yes, those things were interesting. But did you happen to notice the older man selling T-shirts just off the Mall? Did you see how he seemed to have his friends' initials tattooed on his arm along with the American flag? Did you notice the empty look in his eye? It was almost as though he never thought he'd be selling T-shirts in Washington, D.C."

Then someone else asks, "Well, how was New York?" And your friends say, "Oh, it was really interesting." And they describe the frenzied rush of people on Madison Avenue and Wall Street. They compare that with the starkness and emptiness at Ground Zero—how it feels like a giant cavity abruptly cut out of a place so filled with life.

And you say, "Yes, Ground Zero was ominous. In fact, did you happen to see that teenage girl sitting there? She didn't seem to be a tourist but just had a journal that she was writing in. After a while she was joined by a woman that appeared to be her mother—they looked alike. The woman sat beside her and put her arm around her. They just both sat there without saying anything."

As you and your friends talk, you begin to notice a pattern here. You had the same experience together, and yet it seems as if you noticed different things than your friends did. For some reason you were aware of things that others weren't.

We need the perspectives of others in our lives.

The Gospels themselves—Matthew, Mark, Luke, and John—are like four travelers on a journey. Each one (especially John) tends to notice different things. The same is true for the community of believers today. Each of us, through the Holy Spirit, brings special insights to the story of redemption on our planet.

One of the great hallmarks of the Adventist Church has been our Sabbath school time, which allows the body of Christ to enrich one another. By being part of a group, you're saying that you value the perspectives of other people—that they are worth your time. I firmly believe that the stagnancy of the Adventist Church in North America goes hand in hand with the decline of Sabbath school participation among its members.

Other Christian Voices

If there's any article I've taken heat on through the years, it was a piece I wrote called "On Willow Creek" for the *Adventist Review* in 1998. A large congregation outside Chicago, Willow Creek offered church leadership conferences throughout the year, and many Adventists were attending them to get some fresh ideas on reaching lost people. Willow Creek had been especially successful in reaching out to the "unchurched Harrys and Marys" of the world—bringing spiritual seekers to Christ.

In my article I took the position that it was a healthy thing for Adventist Christians to talk with other Christians—not to compromise our identity but to glean new ideas from other followers of Christ. Indeed, borrowing ideas is a major part of our Adventist heritage. Adventist cofounder Ellen White was very gifted at gleaning the good and discarding the bad. At one point she visited a non-Adventist health institute in Dansville, New York, where people smoked, played cards, and gambled. But Ellen didn't bring back those ideas. Instead, she learned many important health principles that would later become part of the Adventist Church's health message. She wrote about applying the "gospel sieve" in our interactions with others: keeping the good, discarding the bad.

But many Adventists were very uncomfortable with the idea of mingling with other Christian believers. Indeed, some church members returned from Willow Creek and, figuratively speaking, took the Adventist nameplate off their church signs. They embraced many of Willow Creek's methods—including friendship evangelism and contemporary worship songs—while distancing themselves from the Adventist message, as though the two were mutually exclusive. It created unnecessary angst and misunderstandings among the Adventist membership.

Several years later, in a remarkably candid self-study, Willow Creek acknowledged that while it had done well in drawing secular people to Christ, it hadn't been successful in teaching them how to mature in their walk with Christ—how to be self-feeders. As I expected, some Adventists quickly pounced on this information, declaring Willow Creek to be a house of cards—never mind the fact that the Adventist Church suffers from many of the same issues, including the fact that surveys indicate that half of our church members admit they don't study the Bible on their own.

So what should our approach be when it comes to exchanging ideas with those outside our faith community? Should we avoid interaction altogether? Or should we mix freely with any group who calls itself Christian? Here's where I draw the line: As long as an individual or group holds up Scripture as the final authority, we should continue to exchange ideas with them. But when they set it aside, we should run like the wind. Incidentally, this principle applies to those inside our church as well as outside.

Keeping a Balance

This brings me to one other issue: becoming too dependent on one spiritual voice. Not long ago I heard about a group of church members who no longer wanted to offer classes centered on a certain woman. Though they acknowledged that she was a strong Christian, they felt that she had come to have too much influence on their church members—as though anything she said was the gospel itself.

The woman they were concerned about was Beth Moore, a Christian teacher whose books and DVD-based seminars have been extremely popular among Christian women.

When I heard this story, I was shocked. My wife and her friends have loved Beth Moore's biblical studies for many years. I've listened to some of them as well—and although I don't agree with everyting Moore advocates, I've found them to be biblically rich. The way these concerned church members were responding to Beth Moore reminded me, with eerie familiarity, how many Adventist church members have responded to Ellen White through the years: "Yes, she's a spiritual writer, but she's become too important."

We must always seek a sense of balance in our Christian walk. No human being can become too important, or we risk putting our own faith in their sinful hands. At the same time, we need to be careful not to throw out the baby with the bathwater. God gives spiritual gifts to people not only for them to be blessed, but for others to be blessed as well.

For the past few years I've been teaching the Bible inductively at our church. In my preparation and teaching I've used many biblical commentaries from Christian authors, including several Adventist authors. But rarely during this period have I referenced Ellen White's work. It wasn't purely intentional—I've simply enjoyed using the in-depth commentaries that explain one verse at a time.

Recently, however, I've begun reading again through Ellen White's Conflict of the Ages Series. After several years away from it, I've been amazed anew by her insights on the life of Christ and the story of redemption. How could a poorly educated woman from the 1800s write so prolifically—and so powerfully? Yes, she borrowed ideas from other sources, but she somehow seemed to accept only the best ones—and she blessed her readers with so many herself. Truly, this woman had a gift.

But Ellen White isn't the only Christian who can bless you. People in your church, in your friendship circles, and in your wider Christian community can have much to offer your spiritual walk. And you have much to give to theirs. With respect and discernment, let's listen to others the way we'd like others to listen to us.

Chapter 8

Meet at the Text:
The Importance of a
Strong Adventist Center

*"All Scripture is God-breathed and is useful for teaching,
rebuking, correcting and training in righteousness, so that the servant of
God may be thoroughly equipped for every good work. In the presence of
God and of Christ Jesus, who will judge the living and the dead,
and in view of his appearing and his kingdom, I give you this charge:
Preach the word; be prepared in season and out of season; correct, rebuke
and encourage—with great patience and careful instruction. For the time
will come when people will not put up with sound doctrine. Instead, to suit
their own desires, they will gather around them a great number of teachers
to say what their itching ears want to hear. They will turn their ears away
from the truth and turn aside to myths" (2 Tim. 3:16-4:4).*

While we must allow room for different perspectives and ideas in our faith community, there must also be a point at which we draw the line. When anything threatens our very scriptural foundation, we risk losing our identity altogether. I believe the most important issue we face in the Adventist Church today is our approach to the authority of Scripture.

During a 10-year period I worked as an editor with two Adventist magazines. At one I felt comparatively liberal, and at the other surprisingly conservative. My feelings had everything to do with the approaches to Scripture that I encountered in each magazine's constituencies.

Adventist Review

My first job out of graduate school was working at the *Adventist Review* magazine at the world church headquarters outside of Washington, D.C. I had great respect for the editors I worked under—William Johnson and his staff—whom I found to be some of the most balanced and gracious people I've ever known. The ministry of the *Review* was bathed in humility and prayer, and I learned much from those spiritual giants.

At the same time, I was often perplexed at how some on the conservative extreme of the Adventist Church disrupted our ability to function at the magazine. We'd run an article on something such as contemporary worship, and we'd get many, many letters, often anonymous, full of criticism drawing not from the Bible but from tradition and, in a very narrow fashion, from the writings of Ellen White and other Adventists.

In the face of all this, it was easy to feel liberal. I didn't think the world was going to end if we used a variety of instruments in worship in the spirit of Psalm 149 or 150, or if a young woman was wearing a friendship band or a purity ring her dad had given her. To be honest, my view of conservatives wasn't that they were appealing to Scripture, but that they were appealing to narrow tradition and to extrabiblical statements pulled from another time and context.

It's like the letter to the editor I recently saw in my hometown newspaper, the Chattanooga *Times Free Press*. A local Adventist explained that our church "interprets the Word of God through the writings of Ellen White." Now, Ellen White is a powerful Christian voice used by God to focus this movement on Scripture, but she didn't understand her role—nor has this movement ever understood it—as our primary interpreter of Scripture.

When I was exposed to such rigidities, it was easy to feel comparatively liberal. At that time, being liberal to me meant appealing only to Scripture as the final authority, not to anyone or anything else. Liberal to me also meant a Hebrew-like willingness to grapple with hard passages for ourselves.

Adventist Today

A few years ago I was asked to be editor of *Adventist Today* magazine. The invitation appealed to me journalistically because I saw it as a chance to tackle issues honestly within the church. I also liked the people I worked with. However, I felt disappointed by some surprising attitudes toward Scripture that I encountered within the *Adventist Today* and *Spectrum* communities. I had been hoping for a climate of "What does the text say?" Instead, I often found one of "Why does the text matter?"

For example, at a time when many young men and women struggling with homosexual tendencies are making courageous decisions to be true to the counsel of Scripture and live lives of abstinence, we're seeing a confusing push in the other direction from Adventist thought leaders. One Adventist religion professor wrote that homosexual practice is "not sin, though it was condemned in Scripture, reflecting apparently the Hebrew understanding of the times." Do you see the line of thought here? He wasn't arguing that the Bible supported the practice of homosexuality. Rather, he was saying that we now understand more than the biblical writers did.

Without question, many of our churches have not been safe harbors for people struggling with homosexuality. People with homosexual temptations need community—and we have shamed and sent them away into communities of darkness. Instead, they should be able to come into the light and find community and support within our churches. We ought to treat gay Adventists who choose abstinence like heroes, considering the burden that they carry. But for paid Adventist leaders to undercut the clear Bible-based teachings of our church on sexual sin is simply irresponsible.

I've also been surprised to see doubts raised about whether Jesus was as knowledgeable as we are. Once in an online discussion about creation and evolution, someone pointed out that both Jesus and Paul had referred to Adam and Eve as literal individuals. The response from an Adventist thought leader? "Of course, Jesus and Paul believed in Adam and Eve. They lived in the first century, and that was their understanding at the time." Do you see what's going on here? Again, it isn't "What does the text say?" but "Why does the text matter?"

In Scripture Jesus also refers to Daniel the prophet. Yet we have Adventist thought leaders saying that there *was* no Daniel the prophet— that someone composed the book of Daniel hundreds of years after the events it prophesies. So in essence, they're arguing that Jesus must not have understood as much about Daniel as they do. Are they sure they want to go down that road? Until recently, scholars also cast doubt on whether a King David existed. Well, now archaeologists are finding extrabiblical evidence for him. Are we not allowed to believe in the biblical text until it's been independently confirmed?

To be honest, I don't really know what to do with this approach to Scripture—the idea that we can set aside its major teachings because we think we understand more now. That seems much different to me, much more dangerous, than grappling with the meaning of a text, as Adventist theologian Desmond Ford once did.

Out of curiosity, I decided to see what Desmond Ford, the controversial figure of Adventism's great theology debate of the 1980s, thought about such things. I e-mailed him in Australia, sharing the above illustrations. Here's what he wrote back: "These examples that you used," he wrote, "present an attitude toward Scripture that the Christian church has repudiated for

2,000 years. These men have given the Word of God a nose of wax. The best of evangelical scholars in other communions would be horrified by these departures."

Do you see the irony here? Years ago we couldn't make room for people who took a high view of Scripture and who were grappling honestly with the biblical text. Yet today we've got church thought leaders willing to set aside major biblical teachings altogether. Incidentally, those aren't dull minds we're talking about here—they're very bright. In fact, they are people who are supposed to be carrying the torch in the deep study of the Word of God. What they seem to forget sometimes is that spiritual things are spiritually discerned. You can't always measure, date, and quantify the Word of God. Instead, you enter into it by faith and by prayer.

Needed: A Strong Adventist Center

We need a strong center again in the Adventist Church: people willing to say, You know what? We can meet at the text. We can grapple with it together. There's enough room here for discussion and different perspectives. As long as you're willing to respect the authority of the Word of God, there's room for you.

In *Sitting at the Feet of the Rabbi Jesus*, Ann Spangler and Lois Tverberg describe what a Jewish seminary is like: "If you crack open the door of an Orthodox Jewish *yeshiva* [seminary] study hall, you might expect to be greeted by utter silence. . . .

"Instead what will greet you is the din of multiple conversations. Pairs of students will be standing at podiums facing each other, animatedly discussing the fine points of each text. Bespectacled students will have one hand poised over an open volume while the other hand gestures wildly, the debate waxing and waning. If one student doesn't understand a passage, the other tries to explain it. Together they think of possible interpretations of the text. This gathering of students is called a *havruta*, and each student is studying with a *haver* (pronounced hah-VAIR; literally a 'friend') to master the text. . . .

"In ordinary usage, the word *haver* can simply mean a companion or a close friend. But here it actually means someone who is willing to partner with you in grappling with Scripture and with the rabbinic texts" (pp. 66, 67).

To our Hebrew forebears, Scripture was life. The Hebrews were known as "people of the ear" because their religion was based not on images of God but on the Word of God. Scripture filled their minds and spilled out into their everyday conversations. The whole life of the Hebrew was *centered* on Scripture.

The Adventist community, too, should be calling people back to Scripture. Our young people should come to our churches and schools and have their minds stuffed with Scripture—and then scatter to the four winds. But for this to happen with our children, we need to be in the text ourselves, so that it's spilling out of our minds, into our lives and everyday speech.

Wrote Jeremiah: "Stand at the crossroads and look; ask for the ancient paths, ask where the good way is, and walk in it, and you will find rest for your souls" (Jer. 6:16).

Chapter 9

Where the Power Is:
Using Scripture in Church,
School, and Evangelism

In a graduate religion class I once took, the professor told about a difficult life period during which his spirit felt empty. One Sabbath he broke from his routine and visited a small, out-of-the-way church pastored by a simple, old man. The old pastor wasn't a dynamic preacher and didn't use contemporary illustrations or visual aids. Nor did he speak on the hot topic of the day. Instead, he led his small congregation, verse by verse, through the deep exploration of a single passage of Scripture. The professor left church that day with his spirit filled.

It is called inductive study or expository preaching—and as both a congregation member and a part-time pastor, I've found it to be the most powerful form of Bible study. During the past two years at my church we have walked verse by verse through the following books together: Ephesians, Ruth, John, Philippians, Daniel, Esther, Ezra, Malachi, Hebrews, and Exodus. Some books took us only a few weeks, while the Gospel of John required seven months.

For a worship service like ours, in which we have a rotation of speakers, such a structure provides needed continuity from the pulpit. But more important, it places the focus on the Word of God rather than on the individual speaker. When the congregation leaves each Sabbath, we want them thinking about the text, not us.

What may surprise some people is that our worship service, called Connect, is considered "contemporary" in style, with praise music, multimedia, and a relaxed feel. People might expect that a congregation such as ours—which includes many youth and university students—would devote its sermons exclusively to the "relevant" topics of the day in order to hold people's attention.

And, yes, periodically we do change things. Topical preaching can be very powerful as well. After all, Jesus Himself preached topically. (Of course, everything He said became Scripture.) Any sermon that's grounded in the Word of God can be used for His glory. The challenge with topical preaching is that it's very difficult in a 30-minute sermon to get to the essence of a biblical passage without the opportunity to explain its background and context thoroughly.

The best way to discover the riches of Scripture is to work prayerfully through it verse by verse, with the aid of the best commentaries and study tools. A straightforward, inductive study doesn't mean the absence of creative elements—not at all. A worship planning team will enjoy supplementing the preaching with fresh approaches. For our Gospel of John series an artistic church member built a towering arch and each week etched a new name for Jesus (the Word, the Healer, the Good Shepherd, and so on) that matched the biblical passage. We also showed corresponding video clips from the *Gospel of John* film, a superb word-for-word portrayal, and, when we reached John 12, dispensed nard perfume throughout the sanctuary. During our Philippians study, we released balloons in the parking lot, symbolizing our joy and freedom in Christ. Then for Exodus we turned the middle aisle into a Red Sea crossing with simulated waves on either side and acted out Exodus 20 at the base of a mountain. We concluded Esther with a celebration of Purim and a Jewish potluck. (One struggling cook joked that she was going to buy a cake and write "Jewish" on it.)

In the inductive preaching model the text drives the topic (meaning that a brain-weary preacher doesn't have to come up with a new topic each week). Routinely we have found ourselves struck by the relevance of the ancient text to our lives today. In Ephesians we find a call to the fullness of life, in the Gospel of John we discover the Jesus of one-on-one encounters, in Philippians we learn how joy and hard times can coexist, and in Daniel we sit back and watch the sovereign hand of Adonai guide the nations—because not everything has to be about *me*.

At a time when half of our church members acknowledge that they don't study the Bible on their own, inductive preaching can help equip them with the tools—and the desire—to self-feed spiritually during the week.

Bible Studies Versus Bible Study

I believe that we should use the inductive study approach in other settings, including our classrooms and evangelistic series.

Many Adventist students grow up in Bible classes that largely feel like fill-in-the-blank sessions. They lead students through a study on, for example, the state of the dead or the Holy Spirit, and using a chain-link system, they'll jump all around their Bibles finding the right text. While useful in some ways, such a method doesn't properly teach students how to examine the context of these texts—or how to study the Bible on their own. It would be much more valuable to guide the students in a careful, inductive approach to a biblical book, such as Mark, 1 Peter, or Daniel.

I feel the same about evangelistic series. We can dazzle visitors with dynamic speakers, PowerPoint slides, and a catchy topic-of-the-night for a few weeks, but what happens when the series is over? It would be a much more valuable investment to show community members how to study the Bible responsibly on their own.

Last summer we planned a mission trip to Mexico, where we would construct a church by day and then lead an evangelistic meeting in the evening. The centerpiece of our meeting would be a short upfront presentation on 1 Peter, followed by a 45-minute roundtable discussion on the text. We couldn't wait to hear the perspectives of our Mexican brothers and sisters on the shared biblical passage, and our hope was that after we left, they would consider to self-feed themselves spiritually. It was with heavy hearts that we had to cancel our trip because of security concerns in Mexico. Perhaps someday we'll be able to fulfill our dream of verse-by-verse evangelism.

Many Christians, including this one, can trace a spiritual awakening to a time when God's Word became "alive and active. Sharper than any doubled-edge sword" (Heb. 4:12).

Chapter 10

The Group Jesus
Didn't Have Much Time For

When Jesus walked our earth, there was one group of people that He simply didn't have a lot of time for.

It wasn't, of course, the down and out: the poor, the sinners, the Samaritans. They not only found a reception with Jesus, but He sought them out.

Nor was it the Pharisees. Jesus had a lot of time for them. He spent hours dialoguing with Pharisees and eating in their homes. Late one evening He plumbed the depths of water and Spirit with a Pharisee. One day He would entrust a Pharisee with the gospel to the Gentiles. Jesus had more in common with the Pharisees than with any other group. True, they could get bogged down in minutiae. Concerned that holiness touched every area of life, they wound up debating whether to eat an egg laid on Sabbath. But Jesus knew what a powerful force for the kingdom the Pharisees could be if their grace ever matched their holiness.

Israel had still other groups. The self-supporting Essenes huddled together in study and purity, perhaps rubbing shoulders with John the Baptist and his then-disciples Andrew and John. The Zealots took their righteous fervor too far—setting back their cause more than helping it— but even a Zealot found a place in Jesus' circle.

No, there was only one group that Jesus didn't have much time for—a group who:

were cultural members of the faith, with no real interest in faith.

clumped near large religious institutions.

put up with religious practice only if it was expedient for them.

didn't believe that God cared about the everyday life of people.

rejected much of Scripture.

denied the resurrection.

were secular and political, arrogant and conniving.

coopted the priesthood and ran the Temple.

Can we understand why Jesus so ferociously cleansed the Temple that the Sadducees were desecrating? Rather than simply leave the faith that they for all practical purposes no longer believed in, the Sadducees tried to drag the faith down with them. Their only remaining interest in religion was power and greed: what they could get out of it. Indeed, when the Romans destroyed the Temple in A.D. 70, the Sadducees ceased to exist.

Jesus didn't have much time for the Sadducees because they weren't serious seekers. When they brought Him their sarcastic questions—"Now then, at the resurrection, whose wife will she be?"(Luke 20:33); "Is it right for us to pay taxes to Caesar or not?" (verse 22)—Jesus saw through their fakery, told them they were "badly mistaken," and walked away.

The problem wasn't questions. Jesus could handle them—in fact, welcomed them. The issue was questions without faith, without any recognition that spiritual things are spiritually discerned.

"Are you not in error," Jesus told the Sadducees, "because you do not know the Scriptures or the power of God?" (Mark 12:24).

Jesus' final parable was for the Sadducees: a story of hardened hearts and the rejection of the prophets (the Scriptures) and ultimately the Son of God. "The stone the builders rejected," Jesus said, "has become the cornerstone. . . . Anyone who falls on this stone will be broken to pieces, but anyone on whom it falls will be crushed" (Matt. 21:42-44).

Jesus used the sober imagery of stoning—with perhaps a subtle final appeal: it's better to be broken than to be crushed.

At the end, Jesus didn't walk away from the Sadducees. He allowed Himself to be bound by them, interrogated by them, slapped and spit on by them. Still, He didn't enter into their faithless queries, didn't say much at all—except name Himself as Christ and King.

This should be the approach we take with those most opposed to Christ—people who want to be religious thought leaders apart from Scriptures or the power of God.

Chapter 11

Opening a Letter to Myself:
The State of Adventist Young Adults

In 2011 I received a letter sent way back in 1997. The letter was written by me . . . to me. Titled "A Letter to Myself (Open in 2011)," I published it in the *Adventist Review,* where I was working as a 26-year-old assistant editor. When I composed it, I never imagined that I'd actually be reading it someday, but sure enough, last year I sat down and did exactly that. Here's the letter:

"Dear Andy:

"Happy fortieth. Hope all's well with Cindy and your two teenagers.

"Speaking of stress, remember back in 1997 when you were worried about the 38 to 50 percent attrition rate among your Adventist peers and frustrated that so many programs and ministries targeting youth and young adults were being planned exclusively by people twice, even three times, their age? Remember that?

"Well, I've got news. Now you're them. That's right, pal—Generation X got old. And because it did, I have a little message for you . . .

"If, by any chance, you currently happen to be sitting on a committee that's planning anything for young people, and if young people aren't well represented on that committee, then recues yourself. That's right—get out of your leather chair, flip on your shirt-button telephone, and invite a young person to take your seat.

"Do this, Andy, not because young people in the year 2011 are necessarily more talented, creative, or even progressive than you are. (Some will be; some won't be.) Instead, do it for the same reason the execs at MTV used to let your generation, the Gen Xers, generate MTV. Because 1997 young people best knew the minds of 1997 young people.

"This doesn't mean, Andy, that the youth and young adults of 2011, the millennials, don't need you. They do need you—desperately. They need you to mentor them, to teach them, to pass on what you've learned about Jesus Christ. But when it comes to planning their programs, step back. Give them ownership. Let them do their thing.

"Because in the struggle to be relevant—to communicate Jesus in their language—you can have the best intentions, but you can't change your birth certificate. Don't forget that."

Wow. Reading this letter after all these years leaves me with several impressions:

1. I certainly was a bold young man, wasn't I? How did the *Adventist Review* staff tolerate me so graciously? The confidence I possessed in my 20s got battered like a floor mat in my 30s.

2. Do I still agree with what I wrote? Yes and no. I'm less focused now on being relevant to contemporary culture—speaking in today's language. My colleague Bill Knott and I used to go back and forth on this—the balance between faithfulness and relevance—and as much as I hate to admit it, he had a point. The simple story of redemption running from Genesis to Revelation (and beyond) will always be relevant.

   I do still think it's important to try to involve young adults in all aspects of church life. And I don't think we're doing much better than we used to do. At the 2010 General Conference session the North American Division sent 240 delegates—with only a few under age 30. Our church leaders are devoted and godly people, but they need to do a better job of letting younger members know that they're wanted. After all, two of the three people who cofounded the Adventist Church—Ellen and James White—were ages 17 and 23, respectively.

3. Am I personally practicing what I preached? Yes and no. At the church in which I serve as a leader we do our best to be multigenerational in all our ministries: from music to outreach to our annual Christmas play. But last year I realized that our 12-member leadership team (which was half male, half female) had no members below age 30. We immediately added three twentysomethings. How quickly (and unintentionally) we can slip from our ideals.

4. From my perspective as a college professor and father, I think the years have changed the dynamic with many Adventist young adults. While in the 1990s our cry was "Give us a piece of the pie," the challenges are different now. Many youth and young adults simply don't seem to care much about church—let alone involvement in it.

Young Adults and Church Leadership

Not long ago I decided to see for myself what my own Adventist college students knew about their church leaders. Not that knowledge of church leaders has anything to do with their spiritual health—but I thought it would be an interesting indicator as to how much engaged they are with the world church. At the time I had 57 students ranging from freshmen to seniors. They came from all parts of the U.S., with a few from other nations. Nearly all the students were Adventist.

I asked them to write the names of the following people: (1) the world church president (then Jan Paulsen), (2) the North American Division president (then Don Schneider), and depending where they were from (3) their union president, (4) their conference president, and (5) their local church pastor. Then I requested the students to try to name something each leader felt strongly about. Here were the results:

Ten out of 57 students knew that Jan Paulsen was the world church president. Two named something that they thought he felt strongly about: world mission and women's ordination.

Four out of 57 students knew that Don Schneider was the North American Division president. Zero named something that he strongly supported.

Fourteen out of 57 students could identify their union president. Five named something that their union president felt strongly about: education, members' opinions, conservatism, support for teachers, missions.

Twenty-one out of 57 students could give the name of their conference president. Seven cited something that their conference president felt strongly about: family, growth of Hispanic churches, biblical conservatism, education, youth, tithing, unity, church planting.

Fifty-three out of 57 students knew the name of their local church pastor. Twenty-four named something that their pastor strongly emphasized: marriage sanctity, family time, sexual purity, health message, member participation, outreach, drums, music, spreading the gospel, using psychology to preach God's character, youth involvement, mission trips, community, prejudice, archaeology.

In reviewing their responses, I thought it appropriate that students would have the most familiarity with their local pastor. Still, the low number of students who could identify their denominational leaders seemed startling. Even more disturbing was their inability to specify what these leaders felt strongly about.

Surely students—and their families—could make a little effort to know their church leaders. (I'm quite confident, for example, that most of them could name the players on their favorite sports team or the actors in their favorite movies.) Indeed, one of my students, Jecsy, described how in her home country of Colombia, her church members knew *all* their leaders. She told how privileged she felt to be part of the worldwide Adventist movement, and how surprised she felt when she moved to the U.S. to find a comparative apathy among young Adventists.

The Bigger Threat: Legalism or Materialism?

So what are the causes of apathy among young adults?

Twenty years ago, when I was in college, I remember thinking that the greatest threat to our church was legalism—that by our works we earned our salvation (or at least held on to it!). I remember a Week of Prayer speaker, Dick Duerksen, coming to campus and preaching passionately about grace. His words seemed like water on parched ground to my friends and me.

During this time I dated a girl who wouldn't eat any dairy or sugar. She said it was for health reasons, but I just knew it was for religious reasons. It actually became a goal of mine to get her to eat sugar. One spring afternoon, when she acknowledged that she had a craving for ice cream, I couldn't get her in the car fast enough to take her to Wendy's for a Frosty. I watched as she ate the first few spoonfuls of ice cream, knowing that she was saved that day by grace alone!

Twenty years later, as a college professor, I no longer think that legalism is the biggest threat to our students. Rather, I think materialism is. Adventist students now are much more culture-savvy than they used to be. They know all the movies and television shows, and they can (and do) access anything in the world via their smartphones.

It's not that all popular culture is bad, but many students are so bombarded by it that they often have little left for spiritual things. I've had conversations with my classes about how immersed in the world they are, and they describe some of their best moments as leaving behind their gadgets and going camping—getting away from it all.

Yet I also get the sense that this new generation is increasingly hungry for truth. There's a saying that on the heels of postmodernism will come fundamentalism—which makes sense when you think about it. A group that grows up without truth, without answers, will hunger and thirst for answers to everything. Adventist pastor John McLarty had a great insight:

that the children of conservative parents need liberal mentors, and the children of liberal parents require conservative ones.

Before they're going to be interested in church involvement, many young adults today first need to be called to reformation—to put away their idols. In fact, many of their Gen X parents require the same thing.

Chapter 12

Your Angel and the Movies

"Whatever is true, whatever is noble, whatever is right, whatever is pure, whatever is lovely, whatever is admirable—if anything is excellent or praiseworthy—think about such things" (Phil. 4:8).

On a recent international flight I noticed that the guy sitting next to me (and hogging the armrest) was watching one of the *Twilight* movies. I hadn't seen any of the *Twilight Saga*—nor had I the least inclination to—but as an Adventist university professor, I'd heard quite a few students buzzing about it, including some students I wouldn't have expected.

At one point during the flight I decided to turn from my own movie—which of course I deemed acceptable—to take a peek at the *Twilight* film and see what it was really like. The story line of *Twilight* (PG-13) is of a young woman who can't resist falling in love with a vampire. Sure enough—the particular scene I viewed showed the woman lying there dead, with the handsome but conflicted young vampire biting on her leg. The scenes that followed were even more graphic and disturbing than I'd expected. When I glanced over again a few minutes later, the woman appeared to have been fully resuscitated and ready to carry on the romance in time for the next film.

Back at my classroom I talked with my students about what I'd seen. "I have an honest question for you," I said. "Why would you want to watch something like that? Do you not think it affects you?"

A couple generations ago Adventist kids heard warnings that if they entered a movie theater, their guardian angel would wait outside. To encourage good choices—as the stories go—some Adventist colleges and academies even positioned employees at the doors of theaters to watch for straying Adventist youth.

How times have changed. No longer do our guardian angels stand waiting at the doors of movie theaters. Now they sit right there with us, munching popcorn.

So how did we tip from one extreme to the other? Here's one scenario:

In the days of "Don't go to a theater," many Adventist youth wondered why it was acceptable to watch the exact same movie (*Chariots of Fire, The Sound of Music, A Cry in the Dark*) a few years later in a school gymnasium or church fellowship hall. If a film was clean, uplifting, even spiritual, why was viewing it in a theater any different? (For the most part, it wasn't—though one can make an argument about the theater environment and certainly about previews of less-desirable films.)

When young people realized that the theater could, in fact, show a decent movie, they said, "Well, that's dumb!" and threw caution to the wind. Eager to distance themselves from the silly restrictions ("They're so legalistic!") of their own youth, this generation ("We're saved by grace alone!") raised kids ill-equipped to discern a good film from a bad one. That's why my college students line up Saturday night for *Twilight* and *The Hunger Games*.

And that's why I believe the greatest threat to most Adventist young people today is not legalism; it's secularism. The pendulum swings back and forth, and right now it's swung hard to the secular. What many young people most need—and in their hearts, most want—is an old-fashioned prophetic call (see Ezra/Nehemiah) to a life of holiness, not in order to be saved but in order to enjoy the fullness of life in Christ.

Some films tell stories worth seeing (wherever we view them). Most don't. With one simple, respectful question, let's call our young people to a high standard in all their life choices: Is this really good enough for you?

Chapter 13

It's Not Just the Economy

*"This [2009] was the second year in which [North American]
tithe fell, and the troubled United States economy was blamed for
much of the shortfall."*—Adventist World, *January 2011, p. 12.*

*"We are budgeting . . . in an economy that's giving us less money
than we need."*—Adventist News Network, *Jan. 18, 2011.*

In the 1992 presidential election Bill Clinton's victory was credited, in part, to a recognition of the pressing issue of the day: the struggling U.S. economy. Riding the slogan "It's the economy, stupid," the Clinton campaign seemed to get it.

The slogan has come to mind, but in a different way, the past few months as I've read explanations of diminished tithe returns in North America. (Tithe has been dropping about 2 percent per year, even though membership has risen by about 2 percent per year.) Everyone seems to attribute the diminished church giving primarily to the struggling U.S. economy.

Now, there's no question that the economy plays some part here. Many church members have seen their wages cut or have lost their jobs altogether. But I'm concerned that we're ignoring the deeper issue: the number of church members who pay only a partial tithe—or none at all.

Here, for example, are the final North American membership and tithe figures for 2009:

2009 membership: 1,101,158
2009 tithe return: $877,932,667
2009 tithe return per member: $821

A tithe return of $821 per member means that, if all the (baptized) church members in North America were paying a full tithe of their income, their average annual income would be $8,200—well below the poverty line of $10,830.

Obviously, not all church members (e.g., newly baptized teenagers, stay-at-home parents, retirees) have full-time incomes. So for the sake of argument, let's assume that only half of the North American baptized membership has a full-time income. That would double the average tithe return per member to $1,640, indicating an average annual income of $16,400—a figure still remarkably low. Is it possible that the average full-time income for a church member is only $16,400? Of course not.

The primary problem with giving in North America isn't that (because of the economy) members contribute less than they used to. Rather, it is that many members aren't giving at all.

What does this mean in practical terms? It results in pastoral hiring freezes, causing district pastors who used to shepherd two churches now must tend three. And it can lead to painful pay and staffing cuts.

Could there be a silver lining in all this? Yes, diminished giving means that the denomination may find itself forced to streamline a four-tier administrative structure that should have been dealt with years ago.

Even so, it would be refreshing to see church leaders, in whatever areas they're leading, stand up and speak squarely to the issue. Rather than blame giving patterns only on the economy, we need to find our voices and call a new generation to commitment—give them something to believe in.

The Adventist Church is not just another denomination. We have plenty of problems, but we have a special calling. Wholistic and Judeo-Christian, we exist to point all peoples to the return of Christ. Our own members need to be reminded of that.

Chapter 14

Homosexuality and the Church

For the Christian the real question isn't gay marriage. Everyone should have the same civil rights. While the state probably shouldn't recognize *any* marriage (a religious institution) and should instead call every union "civil," whatever it's called, it should be available equally.

No, the real question for the church is gay practice, because that is where our Scriptures speak.

Recently I viewed a new feature-length documentary, *Seventh-Gay Adventists*, which explores "the spiritual quests of three subjects who wrestle with the difficult issue of reconciling their religious and sexual identities."

Originally conceived as an "issues" film—with a broad range of perspectives—the project evolved into its final narrative form.

Producers Daneen Akers and her husband, Stephen Eyer, are indeed skilled storytellers, and the film's gentle tone softens its in-your-face title. The subjects of the film include two longtime couples—male-male, female-female—and one new couple: a young man and his boyfriend-turned-fiancé. Viewers find themselves brought into their everyday lives—grocery shopping, making supper, family worship, Sabbath school—in a way that feels all too familiar, if not mundane. The message is clear: gay couples are pretty much like anyone else, and our churches should welcome and love them, not leave them out in the cold. The film's most iconic scene is the wedding dance of the two young men, with their loving but conflicted family members looking on. "This has been a journey for us as well," remarks one of the young men's fathers, a church official. "This isn't what we'd imagined for David."

What this film does very well is help the viewer see gay people as . . . people. Those six Adventists aren't just gay—they're also smart and funny and kind (and though the film doesn't depict this nearly enough, they have relationship challenges just as you and I do). At the screening I attended, the room was filled with emotional people who clearly resonated with the three stories told on screen.

But I found myself wishing for a fourth story—the one in which an Adventist loves the same sex, but loves Scripture even more. In 2009 Wayne Blakely—an Adventist who, after 37 years in a gay lifestyle, recommitted his life to Christ and chose celibacy—asked the producers if they would include his story in the film. "It seemed apparent," he writes on his Web site, knowhislove.com, "that they were not seeking any testimonies from same-sex-attracted individuals who have been redeemed and are choosing to live sexually pure through Christ."

When I asked the filmmakers why they didn't portray a celibate gay Adventist, Akers said that they ultimately decided that the film's focus should be on gay Adventists whose lifestyles were in *conflict* with the church's position—because conflict is what makes a story. So there isn't enough conflict in a celibate gay Adventist whose flesh and spirit wage war daily? whose courageous scriptural stance flies in the face of contemporary culture? Ironically, it's still gay Adventists being left out in the cold—except now it's those who choose sexual purity.

Blakely's isn't the only voice of purity. His Web site links to other "redeemed" (their preferred term) Adventist men and women who have put their eternal destinies ahead of short-term tendencies. (A beautiful new memoir, *Out of a Far Country*, by a gay man, Christopher Yuan, and his mother, Angela, also shouts purity from the shelves of mainline bookstores.) Those stories are the truly heroic ones. Not to include even one of them belies this film's more subtle message: the acceptance of the gay lifestyle.

Akers and Eyer say that they are supportive of gay relationships, as long as they're committed and monogamous. "How could a God of love," says Eyer, "ask people not to be in a loving relationship?" It's a hard question that more and more Adventists are sincerely asking. But God is a deity of not only love but also holiness, and He calls us to both during our sojourn on our sin-plagued planet. The Jesus who lovingly told the woman of John 8:11, "Neither do I condemn you" also lovingly told her, "Go now and leave your life of sin."

When any of us struggles with a sinful tendency (as we all do), the last thing we need is for those entrusted with Scripture itself to say, "Go now and *continue* your life of sin." Which of the other tendencies (along with homosexual practice) named in passages such as Romans 1 and 1 Timothy

1 would supporters of a gay lifestyle also encourage struggling people to live out? Greed, envy, murder, strife? Gossip, slander, insolence, arrogance? Adultery, lying, slave trading? Though these behaviors obviously vary in degree (just as those named in the Ten Commandments do), they're still all identified by the Word of God as sin. Why is it only this sinful tendency that's now OK to practice? Because it doesn't hurt anyone else? Or because it hurts only those who practice it?

Chapter 15

When There's Not an Easy Answer

Some countries and cultures around the world still accept the practice of polygamy. It remains common in Kenya, for example, and once a woman is married, she is financially dependent on her husband. Thus the issue has presented a dilemma for the Christian church (and not just the Mormon Church). What should be done when members of a polygamous marriage—either a man or one of his wives—becomes a Christian?

The official Adventist Church policy when a husband becomes a believer is for the husband to keep his primary wife and to financially support the secondary wives and children while no longer living with them. But when a secondary wife becomes a member, the situation is much more complicated. For a woman in Kenya, it's difficult to provide for herself and her children on her own. Also, many married women love and have formed an attachment to their husband and don't want to have to choose between marriage and Christianity.

Recently an Adventist pastor from the United States, John Nixon, gave a series of talks in Nairobi, Kenya. At one of the meetings Pastor Nixon made an altar call, and among those who responded was a woman who was a secondary wife. As the respondents walked from the altar back to the prayer room, the elders of the church pulled the woman out of the line because they knew her situation and would not let her join with the others who wanted to be baptized.

The woman came to see Pastor Nixon the next day and told him her story. Her parents had given her to her sister's husband because her sister was barren. At an early age she married him and had four children with him. Later her sister became pregnant too, but the younger sister was always the husband's favorite. In addition, the woman's daughter was distraught at the prospect of her home being broken up. She wanted her mother to be baptized, but she didn't want to lose her home. Now the local church was requiring her mother to break up her home in order to join herself to Christ. It was a horrible dilemma.

How should the church handle the situation? Should it allow the woman to be baptized even if she stays in the marriage as a secondary wife?

The situations we get ourselves into. Like a tangled web.

Another Dilemma

Our contemporary dilemma with polygamy is similar, in some ways, to another marriage dilemma the Jews faced long ago. After their captivity in Babylon many of them returned to Jerusalem intent on not making the same mistakes their ancestors had. In particular, the Jews determined to avoid falling into idolatry or worshipping other gods. And that's why these Jews were particularly turned off by what had been happening in the northern part of the country—Samaria.

After the destruction of the northern kingdom of Israel, its conquerors settled foreign peoples in Samaria who intermarried with the remaining Israelites there. In some cases Israelite husbands even appear to have divorced their own wives to marry pagan women. All the intermarriages between Israelites and pagans created a mixed people that became known as Samaritans.

The problem with such marriages wasn't that the new people were foreign. God had made accommodation for non-Israelites who wanted to become part of Israel and worship Yahweh. Many important spouses in Israel's history were foreigners. Ruth the Moabite married Boaz. The wives of both Joseph and Moses were non-Israelites who became believers in Yahweh.

The problem wasn't that the women in Samaria were foreign—rather, that they were pagan. They had brought with them pagan gods and weren't willing to let them go. So the Jews in Jerusalem despised the newly mixed people up north because they blended worship of Yahweh with worship of pagan deities.

Ezra 4 tells how the Samaritans offered to help rebuild the Temple in Jerusalem. The leaders in Jerusalem basically told them, "Get lost. Go back home to Samaria." Ultimately it led to the Samaritans' constructing their own temple on their own mountain, called Mount Gerizim, where Jacob had once settled. The Samaritans then claimed that it was the true mountain of the Lord. Yet how could the Samaritans at one point say that they wanted to help build the Temple of the Lord in Jerusalem and then, after being rebuffed, say that the true temple of the Lord was in Samaria on Mount Gerizim?

Naturally, the Jews down south didn't want anything to do with the Samaritan lifestyle, in which believers in Yahweh married pagan spouses. They regarded it as abhorrent. And that's why the events described in Ezra 9 and 10 were so deeply embarrassing.

Close to Home

"After these things had been done, the leaders came to me and said, 'The people of Israel, including the priests and the Levites, have not kept themselves separate from the neighboring peoples with their detestable practices, like those of the Canaanites, . . . Moabites, Egyptians and Amorites. They have taken some of their daughters as wives for themselves and their sons, and have mingled the holy race with the peoples around them. And the leaders and officials have led the way in this unfaithfulness'" (Ezra 9:1, 2).

What the Jews most despised about others they had now become guilty of themselves. Have you ever experienced that? What you can point out so easily, so judgmentally in others, you find yourself guilty of?

I have this strange phrase in my head sometimes. I don't know where I heard it from. It isn't in Scripture. Maybe it was a sermon. The phrase is: "I'm going to make you sit where they sat." I think it is about being humbled, about not being too quick to judge. *I'm going to make you sit where they sat.* That's what's happening here.

Some of the Jewish leaders—even the priests themselves—had married pagan women and had children with them. It wasn't a large group, perhaps only 100 or 200 out of a population of 30,000 in Judah. Still, it had a big emotional effect on the people. The Jews wanted their land to be free from such things, to be pure, without any hint of the outside world.

Once I was reading about the early days of Disney World. Walt Disney didn't want people who visited Disney World to be able to see anything but Disney World. When you're on a ride at Disney, even the high ones, you're not able to view anything outside of the amusement park. It's all part of the sensory experience, the aesthetics. You can't discern the interstate or Orlando. All you can see from Disney is Disney.

The Jews wanted Jerusalem to be like Disney: all you can perceive from Jerusalem is Jerusalem. The Jews didn't want a hint of the outside world. And then, suddenly, they found themselves infiltrated in the most personal of ways by paganism. Tearing his cloak, Ezra sat all day thinking about how to handle the situation. If you were the one in charge, what would you do?

Ezra was a gentle and respected leader, and commentators have noted that here he didn't immediately berate the people. Instead, he took some time to ponder the dilemma prayerfully and decide what to do.

One of Ezra's counselors suggested that he should send away all the pagan women and children. We might call it the "cleanse the temple" approach. There's certainly a place to cleanse the temple. If you have a chemical addiction, you need to cleanse the temple—to detox. Or if you're filling your personal temple with junk, you need to sterilize it with soap and water and the blood of the Lamb. There are institutions, many of them self-supporting, that specialize in cleansing the temple—in separating from any hint of the world. We should be careful not to judge such places too quickly, though. People need different things at different seasons of life. But the "cleanse the temple" approach gets much more complicated when it involves real people who have become family members: spouses and children.

Ultimately, after a season of prayer and soul-searching, Ezra indeed followed this path. He asked the men of Israel to separate themselves from their foreign wives and children. (Ezra 10)

People interpret what happened here in different ways. I have heard these male Jewish leaders described as lunatics who severely overreacted: sending away wives and children. Others take the text as a hard but necessary experience: God wanted a holy people free from pagan influences, and the intermingling of God's people with pagans threatened the long-term identity of the Jews. Commentator F. C. Holmgren writes: "A covenant community that allows its *leaders* to adopt a lifestyle that threatens the central covenant . . . is sacrificing its future."

In *Prophets and Kings* Ellen White writes: "With infinite patience and tact, and with a careful consideration for the rights and welfare of every individual concerned, Ezra and his associates strove to lead the penitent of Israel into the right way" (p. 622).

It's a very difficult image: wives and children being driven away, sent to the mixed populations of Samaria. The fact that it doesn't feel *good* to us is another indicator of the broken, messed-up world that we live in: one today still rife with agonizing dilemmas and bitter tears, children reaping the consequences of their parents' poor decisions. How these late Old Testament men and women required a Messiah. And how we ourselves still need a Messiah.

An Unexpected Visitor

And that's why seven words in the New Testament are so meaningful when we understand their context. We find those seven words in the Gospel of John: "Now he had to go through Samaria" (John 4:4).

Jesus of Nazareth was traveling north from Jerusalem back home. The text says, "He had to go through Samaria," but that wasn't really true in a physical sense. The Jews hardly ever went through the region. Instead, they crossed the Jordan River and circled around Samaria.

While Jesus didn't have to travel through Samaria physically, He had to do so spiritually. The Samaritans were His children too, and He loved them—a shepherd seeking out the lost sheep of Israel. On this day Jesus would show the extent of His love to a mixed-up Samaritan woman who had descended from a mixed-up intermarried people. Having been married to five men and now living with a sixth, she was such an outcast that even the other Samaritans rejected her. That's apparently why she was drawing water not at her local well but instead from a more isolated one a half mile away: Jacob's well.

Jesus had to go through Samaria. Perhaps the Jewish people before Jesus weren't ready for encounters like these. Maybe they couldn't handle them. But Jesus could. He had now come to bind up the broken pieces—to make all things new.

"When a Samaritan woman came to draw water, Jesus said to her, 'Will you give me a drink?' (His disciples had gone into the town to buy food.)

"The Samaritan woman said to him, 'You are a Jew and I am a Samaritan woman. How can you ask me for a drink?' (For Jews do not associate with Samaritans.)

"Jesus answered her, 'If you knew the gift of God and who it is that asks you for a drink, you would have asked him and he would have given you living water'" (John 4:7-10).

Chapter 16

The Other Way to Feel Empty

" 'Sir,' the woman said, 'you have nothing to draw with and the well is deep. Where can you get this living water?' " (John 4:11).

As part of my doctoral program I read more than 40 memoirs—formative periods of a person's life. Along with the classic memoir writers—Elie Wiesel, Tobias Wolff, Frank McCourt, Annie Dillard, Russell Baker—I read a variety of contemporary writers, from the very secular to the very spiritual, all individuals who tried to make sense of their lives:

Augusten Burroughs, whose lifestyle of alcohol and immorality keeps a talented writer from being what he could be.

Elizabeth Andrew, a bisexual writer who grew up Christian but who now broadens the sacred to include all religions—as well as Stonehenge.

Kim Barnes, so desperate to get away from a heavily conservative Pentecostal upbringing that she panted at almost everything else. "Better to risk body and soul," she wrote, "than to be imprisoned by the tyrannical laws my father and the church imposed. I was hungry for a world I had never known, . . . I spent my fourteenth year in basements and back alleys, in the blue glow of black lights, listening to Led Zeppelin, learning how to French-kiss, smoking dope, dropping mescaline, waiting for a vision that might change it all."

A beautiful girl, Barnes got so heavily involved in sex that it became her whole identity. When a guy didn't get intimate at the end of a date, she felt as if he had rejected her whole person. Eventually she gave herself over to a truck driver who took her to seedy locations and rented her out to other drivers. By the end of her story, she had summoned the courage to boot him out, restore a healthy relationship with her parents, and find a wholesome faith and marriage.

What struck me profoundly about such stories was the absence of fulfillment apart from God and the godly life.

When I turn from the harder stories back to those I find in the church, it's of course sad but not surprising to see plenty of familiar images: sex outside of marriage, recreational drinking, gambling (in all its forms), greed, career over kids, panting after pop culture, embracing other gods.

What disturbs me isn't the presence of sin in the church (not exactly a headline), but what seems to be a changing attitude toward sin—whether it's confessed or celebrated. When Paul sent his first letter to Corinth (a church of probably 55 members), he expressed exasperation not just at the sin but at the laissez-faire attitude toward sin: "A man has his father's wife. And you are proud!" (1 Cor. 5:1, 2).

That's the sense I'm getting more and more. It used to be that when church members sinned, we at least felt bad about it—or if they didn't feel guilty, they at least left the faith community. Now some of us are doing neither. We're sticking around, even taking leadership roles, with an arrogance matched only by those who think we can earn our way to eternal life.

What both groups—legalists and libertines—have in common is a looking to self for fulfillment. Both groups take a low view of the Scriptures that teach we find neither joy nor worth outside of a biblically grounded life in Christ.

Everything else is a merry-go-round around a merry-go-round around a merry-go-round. Everything else is a well that never satisfies.

"Jesus answered, 'Everyone who drinks this water will be thirsty again, but whoever drinks the water I give them will never thirst. . . .'

"The woman said to him, 'Sir, give me this water so that I won't get thirsty and have to keep coming here to draw water'" (John 4:13-15).

Chapter 17

Three Ideas for Your Church

Through the years I've benefited so much from the fresh ideas of other believers. Here are three ideas I'd like to share with you.

A Sabbath Plaza for Your Community

Jesus told us to be two things: the salt of the earth and a light on a hill. Being the salt of the earth means bringing the message of Christ to the people. Being a light on a hill involves leading the people to the message.

After witnessing the beautiful sense of community on Friday evenings at the Temple Mount plaza in Jerusalem (see chapter 2), I asked myself: What if our Adventist churches back home created their own gathering place on Friday evening—a place so beautiful, so inviting, that even people outside our faith community would want to come and experience it—or at least drive by slowly? Its purpose wouldn't be to mimic the Temple plaza— which has a deep meaning all its own. Rather, in our own significant way, we would celebrate our salvation rest in Christ with the arrival of Sabbath rest—in an Eden-like oasis from the noise of secular culture.

Here in Collegedale, Tennessee, where I live, we're developing a Sabbath plaza where people can gather Friday evening to enjoy fellowship, pray, discuss Scripture, eat a picnic supper, Hebrew dance—whatever their hearts desire. In many ways such an environment is reminiscent of the beautiful community we find in Acts 2, in which the early Christians "devoted themselves to the apostles' teaching and to the fellowship, to the breaking of bread and to prayer. . . . Every day they continued to meet together in the temple courts" (Acts 2:42-46).

What might a Sabbath plaza in your community look like? That's the fun part: creating it together with our individual communities in mind. Maybe it's full of fountains and flowers. Perhaps there are warmers in the ground for the winter. It could have a special prayer tree, a water altar, or an area where people stand face to face at podiums to discuss Scripture, like a

Jewish *havruta*. Or it could include an outdoor baptismal spot. Whatever the specifics, it should be one of the most beautiful places around—a light on a hill that draws all kinds of people.

Remember: this wouldn't be a program. We have enough of them in our churches. Instead, it would be a place where spiritual community happens spontaneously and naturally. What kind of place would you and your friends and your family look forward to going to on Friday evening—to celebrate Christ, to break free from secular culture, to welcome Sabbath with friends new and old? My e-mail address is andynash5@gmail.com. I'd love to hear from you.

A New Way to Observe Foot Washing

Recently at our church we observed the foot-washing ordinance in a different way, based on our study of Jesus' preparing His disciples to be new covenant priests by symbolically cleansing their feet. (See chapter 5: "Jesus of Nazareth—The Treasure of Heaven".)

First, we decided to keep foot washing close to the Lord's Supper table itself, as Jesus did, rather than send the congregation out of the sanctuary. Before the members walked forward to pick up the bread and grape juice, we invited them to leave their shoes and socks at their seats. We had set up eight foot-washing stations at the front of the sanctuary—four on each side.

As the church members approached the Communion table, they had the option of briefly sitting at a foot-washing station, where an attendant would wash their feet with a fresh towel dipped in a basin. The attendant then spoke a short blessing: "May the God of peace . . . equip you with everything good for doing his will" (Heb. 13:20, 21). The members then picked up the bread and juice and returned, barefoot, to their seats for the Lord's Supper. Quiet music and low lighting provided a reverent atmosphere for the experience.

Many church members said how much they appreciated the close linking of the foot washing with the Lord's Supper and that it reminded them of their priestly calling in the new covenant of Christ. It also removed some of the awkwardness of sending people to another room to find a foot-washing partner.

Perhaps the biggest downside was that only eight people had the privilege of washing people's feet. Some members missed performing the service. Next time we plan to set up many more chairs up front, with stacks of fresh towels and buckets of water. It will give members the choice of having their feet washed by an attendant (as we did this time) or pairing up with a friend. Both will happen on the way to the Lord's Supper table. "May the God of peace . . . equip you with everything good for doing his will."

The Only Advice I'll Ever Give About Fellowship Meals

You don't need juice and soda at a fellowship meal (also called a "potluck" or "covered dish meal"). Ice water is sufficient and much less hassle. Place pitchers filled with ice water at each table about 10 minutes before the meal begins.

The tables should have tablecloths. No one wants to look at a room full of bare tables. You can purchase tablecloths (polyester and permanent press) in quantity. Watch for sales or coupons. A few different sets would be best—checkered, white pastels, red for holidays, etc. Set the tables nicely with paper napkins, white disposable plates, clear plastic cups turned upside down on the napkin, and plastic silverware. A nice table setting shows guests how important they are to the church family. Each table should have two table hosts who make sure everyone at their table gets acquainted and knows what to do.

Arrange the serving tables in the shape of a cross (with the crossbeam in the center). In this formation, the lines can extend on both ends and on both sides—saving time and keeping people happy. Place the desserts on the middle (crossbeam) table; next, the salad, veggies, and breads on either side; and finally—immediately after the blessing—the hot dishes on the outside. Put serving spoons on both ends of each dish so that people can easily reach a dish that isn't on their side of the table. To guard against hoarding, cut each dessert and put the pieces on small, separate plates, e.g., one slice of pie, one piece of cake, one or two cookies.

You may begin without a pastor who gets delayed. Have the blessing and then dismiss the tables one at a time. Don't call too many tables at once, and don't always start with the same table, the reason being obvious.

If someone shows up for the dinner and you know they didn't bring a dish, don't say anything. Just let it go. (No gossiping in the kitchen whatsoever.) If you're certain that you're going to be short on food, announce it tactfully beforehand, asking everyone to limit their portions.

Should a dear old man keep coming into the kitchen to help, tell him that everything seems to be running smoothly but that you could use his help afterward with cleanup and taking leftovers to the sick or needy.

If some of the team members are constantly bickering in the kitchen, the team leader should talk to them privately, affirming them both but laying down the law. The team leader must be fully empowered to run the dinner as she or he sees fit. Occasionally surprise the team members with little gifts, candies, or notes of appreciation. It will gain their everlasting loyalty.

The fellowship team should meet regularly to evaluate their most recent dinners against their fellowship dinner mission statement and to create a bond of unity. Welcome critiques and suggestions, and take and keep minutes. You can also use the meeting to plan future fellowship meals. Consider possible themes and accompanying decorations, e.g.: January—snowmen, February—hearts, March—kites. Colorful napkins can readily carry a theme.

OK, OK, confession time. I actually don't know very much about fellowship meals. All these ideas came from my grandmother, Margaret Nash, who died this past year. Grandma practically lived for fellowship meals: early in her life praying for the gift of hospitality and, when she received it, blessing tens of thousands with it.

Before Grandma died, my mom interviewed her extensively—collecting all her wisdom for a new generation. Grandma once remarked that she felt Martha got a "bum deal."

Chapter 18

The Church of Awesome

My family and I got a good laugh when we came across *The Book of Awesome: Snow Days, Bakery Air, Finding Money in Your Pocket, and Other Simple, Brilliant Things*, by Neil Pasricha. This fun book is devoted to the "most awesome things in life." Here were some of our favorite entries:

◎ when you push the button for the elevator and it's already there
◎ waking up before your alarm clock and realizing you've got lots of sleep time left
◎ popping bubble wrap
◎ the final seconds of untangling a really big knot
◎ scraping all the lint off an overflowing lint trap
◎ the thank-you wave from the driver you let merge in front of you
◎ when you're about to fall asleep and someone throws a blanket on you
◎ when your dad pushes you off and you ride your bike for the first time
◎ picking up a Q and a U at the same time in Scrabble
◎ the moment at a restaurant when you see your food coming
◎ that one square in the waffle that's most loaded with butter and syrup
◎ hanging your hand out the car window
◎ moving up a shoe size when you're a kid
◎ the three-paycheck (five, if paid weekly) month
◎ building an amazing couch-cushion fort
◎ squeezing through a door as it's shutting without touching it
◎ slipping in the bathtub but catching yourself at the last second (And here I thought I was the only one who did that.)

So what about church life? Any awesome things there? With help from my awesome family, here's a start:

◎ when the tall person sitting in front of you decides to move down the row

◎ when you and your friend both come in too early on the next line of the song

◎ when you walk into Sabbath school and people look happy to see you

◎ when the baby being dedicated grabs at the microphone

◎ the congregation's second response to the double "Good morning!"

◎ when someone brings Oreo Mint Dessert to potluck and your table gets called first

◎ nailing your memory verse

◎ Aunt Sue and Uncle Dan

◎ church roller-skating night

◎ seeing someone walk into church who hasn't come for a long time

◎ getting a new insight on a scripture you've heard all your life

◎ still remembering the numbers of songs in *Advent Youth Sing*

◎ when the dozing elder up front suddenly wakes with a start

◎ handing out flowers for Mother's Day Sabbath

◎ the key change in "How Great Thou Art"

◎ when someone you've been studying with asks about baptism

◎ going back and forth between "Hallelu, Hallelu, Hallelu, Hallelujah" and "Praise ye the Lord"

Chapter 19

My Generation Is Better
Than Your Generation

I once asked a group of 25 Adventist college students (born 1987-1989) a simple question: If you had a choice, would you rather have grown up when you actually did, or grow up when your kids will? Clinton was the first president they remember. Generally speaking, their kids will be born during the next few years.

Of the 25 students, a total of zero said they would want to grow up in the next generation (that of their own kids). Even when I reminded them of the advances in technology and medicine, they held firm. They wouldn't want to grow up in the 2010s and 2020s. No way, they said, shaking their heads in unison.

"Why not?" I asked.

"Everything's gotten so materialistic," one young woman said.

"It's as if all kids want to do is play video games," another added.

"But that's what everyone thinks about your generation!" I protested.

"At least we knew how to play outside," one guy protested. "And we were more family-centered than kids are now."

"So you're saying the culture is going downhill," I suggested.

Yes, they replied. Things are getting worse.

"OK," I continued, "we've gone about 25 years into the future, and you're saying it's worse. Let's go 25 years the other way." I wrote a couple of dates on the board: 1962 and 1937. "This is when your parents and grandparents were born. How many of you would rather have grown up when they did?"

The students paused, and some of them smiled.

"How many?" I repeated.

Three students raised their hands—two of them confidently, one not so sure.

"Three. A total of three of you would rather have grown up in your parents' or grandparents' generation. That leaves 22 of you preferring to grow up when you did."

I paused for a few seconds. "You know what you're saying, don't you? You're claiming that you grew up at the perfect time in history. Things were gradually improving until your time. Then everything fell apart."

We all laughed. I told them that I probably would have answered the same way. After all, I loved the era in which I grew up: the eighties. Without a doubt, the music of the late eighties (my high school years) is the greatest music of all time. And eighties clothing styles are still the coolest too.

It's true. Most of us view "our era" as the perfect balance between yesterday and tomorrow. Life was still "simple," and yet we had the modern conveniences that we couldn't imagine living without. For me it was a personal computer. For my students it has been e-mail and cell phones.

Then we talked about the attributes of each generation. "Let's take your grandparents," I said. "Chances are, they're very patriotic people. Very loyal to their country and to their churches. Right?" The students nodded.

"They were hardworking, and they were frugal. They had come out of the Depression. They have a lot of excellent qualities."

I paused. "And they might be racist. To this day some of them still carry racist attitudes."

The expressions changed as students recognized the truth of the statement when applied to their own grandparents and other relatives—perhaps a shocking offhand remark made at the holiday dinner table.

It's natural to feel loyalty to our generation—to the good as well as the bad. Grandma and Grandpa were no different. As children of the thirties and forties, they saw how to be patriotic—and how to be racist.

Generational loyalty can be just as much a problem for the rest of us. While college students today tend to be less racist than those who went before them, their generation tends to have its own problems, including a sense of entitlement and disrespect for authority.

"The challenge each of us faces," I said, "is to keep the good and throw out the bad." For some of us, that can be as hard as admitting that those cool college clothes . . . just aren't cool anymore.

Chapter 20

Older Men Who Feel Stuck

"For though a righteous man falls seven times,
he rises again" (Prov. 24:16).

There's a guy I occasionally see who's now in his 50s. I knew him when he was in his 30s. As a kid, I looked up to him and in many ways wanted to be like him. He was an extremely gifted spiritual leader, a devoted father and husband, and a fun, all-around person.

But now, years later, the man has changed—not only in appearance, but also in other ways. He still has the same wit, the same affection for people. But his words and actions reveal a diminished interest in spiritual things.

I asked one of his family members about him. What had happened to all that spiritual giftedness—the promise so many of us saw?

"He's just stuck," the family member said. Years earlier the man had made some personal mistakes that were very difficult to come back from.

I've crossed paths with others like him—older individuals who feel stuck, who no longer know what to do with themselves. I once met a 70-something man who, years ago, was an American celebrity. He appeared on television with a pony he'd taught to do tricks. In time the show's popularity faded, until it was finally canceled. Without his former identity, the man became lost, bitter, and broke. In desperation, in his *70s* he was trying to train a new pony and recapture the magic from another time and place. It was painful to watch.

But not all men have to go down this road. There's another type of older man out there—one who ages gracefully, who accepts that the former things are gone, who doesn't cling to his old identity but embraces a new one: patriarch.

They are the Jacobs, the Moseses, the Davids of our day—men who have made mistakes (as all human beings have) but don't let those mistakes determine the rest of their lives. The thing about David—the reason he's called a man after God's own heart—is that he just wouldn't give up. After such a promising start, David faded too—became an adulterer, murderer, lousy father. But he just kept coming back from darkness into light. "I was young and now I am old," he counseled in Psalm 37:27. "Turn from evil and do good; then you will dwell in the land forever."

Our world needs older men committed to doing good for the rest of their days.

When I took my first job at the Adventist church world headquarters, an older man used to come by my cubicle just to see how I was doing. He was so unassuming, so humble, that I found myself surprised to learn he was a vice president of the world church: Phil Follett. I felt honored that Elder Follett would take an interest in me, and the more I heard about him, the more I respected him. A colleague of mine once described boarding a flight and seeing Phil sitting there in an aisle seat, already reading his Bible.

After he retired, Phil moved to Collegedale, Tennessee, where I'd spot him crashing around in his '96 Volkswagen Jetta, always on the go. Five days a week he helped prepare Christian programming for LifeTalk Radio. He loved getting Adventist college students on the air. Phil had a big, big heart for young people—the future of the church that he loved so dearly.

A widower of 26 years and cancer survivor, Phil Follett had every reason to feel stuck. Instead, he gave and gave until he couldn't give anymore. When he died, those close to him learned of many other ways he'd been quietly ministering—many other people whose lives he had touched.

God needs modern-day patriarchs to help bring His children home.

Chapter 21

Remembering to Laugh

I laughed (sort of) when an *Adventist Review* magazine reader once took me to task for one of my column topics. In a letter to the editor, a woman named Susan from San Diego wrote: "I read Nash's column Growing Up Adventist back in the nineties, and I have to admit that it captured my attention much more than his current fascination with biblical interpretation. Is the Sabbath in Colossians 2 something that actually comes up in everyday conversation?"

My first reaction when I read her letter was to say, "Well!" But as I thought more about it, I felt grateful for the reminder about balance in the Christian life.

At different stages we're naturally going to have different interests. When I was younger, I enjoyed writing humor stories about growing up Adventist. But as I got older, my interests changed. What can I say? I grew up. (It reminds me of a trip we took to an amusement park. For some reason I still possessed an old, tattered children's pass with my name on it. It had a few punches left, but now I was too old to use it. At the ticket window, I told the woman, "I got this pass when I was a kid, but I grew up." She laughed and swapped it for an adult pass.)

The past few years I've found myself more interested in deeper topics—inductive Bible study and theology. I wrote that article on Colossians 2 because I thought it was relevant to church members whose family members and friends were raising questions about the Sabbath.

But I was glad for the reminder about variety—even levity—in the Christian life. It's easy when any of us gets excited about something to overdo it. (Oh, there's Dave. We all know what *he's* going to talk about.) We need to be careful not to pigeonhole ourselves by beating the same drum all the time. Also, we must remember to laugh a little. My own daughters, for example, hardly ever tell me that their friends like me because I am interested in biblical interpretation. But they do say that their friends appreciate me because I make them laugh.

In fact, one of the things I've enjoyed learning in my (shhh!) biblical studies is that a major part of Jewish life centered on joy and laughter. That's right. "A time to laugh" was central to the life of faith. God's people knew how to feast—to have good, clean fun. Jesus, our ultimate example, drew all kinds of people into His circle. One minute He was captivating the teachers of the law, while the next minute He was the life of the party—in the best sense of the phrase. That's pretty amazing.

As sober as life can be, when we don't make space for pleasure in our homes and churches, our kids will look for it elsewhere. Although we need times of solemnity and study, we also must have opportunities for levity and laughter—all generations playing together.

So with appreciation for Susan's reminder, I thought I'd share a few of the funnier moments my family, friends, and I have experienced the past few years on our own unpredictable walks of faith.

A Time to Laugh

One day when our daughters were little, I walked into the house to find my wife mockingly pounding her head against the kitchen wall while laughing hysterically.

"I'm such a total idiot," she said.

"What happened?" I asked.

Cindy said she'd just left a phone message with Pam, a woman in town who had offered us a free kitten. For the past few days my wife had been debating whether we should accept the kitten. The girls were only 3 and 1, and Cindy already felt as if she were herding cats. After carefully considering it—even praying about it—she decided it just wasn't the right time for a kitten.

"So I call Pam and leave a message," Cindy said. "I said, 'Hi Pam, this is Cindy Nash. I'm just calling to thank you for the offer of a free kitten. We really thought long and hard about this, but with the girls still so young, I just decided that I'm not up to a kitten right now. I really hope that you can find a good home for the kitten. In Jesus' name, amen."

I laughed. "You really said that? 'In Jesus' name, amen'?"

"Yes!" she screamed. "How could I do that?"

"Then what did you do?"

"Well, I just paused a second, and then I said, 'Um, this is still Cindy here. I'm not sure why I just said, 'In Jesus' name, amen,' but I hope you find a good home for the kitten. Bye!"

At the close of a sermon series on Esther, our church decided to have an Esther drama and Purim celebration. As part of the program, one of our elders suggested that I put on his prayer shawl and recite a traditional Hebrew prayer. The idea sounded great to me until I accidentally pulled the prayer shawl too far down on my face. Not only did I have great difficulty reading the Hebrew prayer, but I had the sense that I looked completely ridiculous.

My feelings were confirmed the following Monday morning. As I began class, one of my students suddenly burst out laughing and said, "Oh, I'm sorry, Dr. Nash, but that was just too funny!"

A friend of ours, Jennifer Woody, told us about a time in her teenage years when she was desperate to use the women's restroom at church. Flying down the hallway, Jennifer rushed into the restroom, flung open the stall door, spun around, and sat down just in time to hear someone meekly say, "Excuse me, this seat is already taken." It was an elderly male voice.

Several years ago when my friend Chris Blake was finishing up his book *Searching for a God to Love*, his publisher, Pacific Press, asked him to help provide some testimonials for marketing materials. He solicited testimonials from carefully selected figures, and then, as he received them, he e-mailed them to Pacific Press using his wife Yolanda's e-mail account. (At the time Chris didn't have an e-mail account.)

A few weeks later Chris opened the *Adventist Review* magazine and was delighted to see a full-page book promotion that included several testimonials from people Chris had contacted. However, he began to feel his blood boil when he saw that one of the testimonials was attributed to someone named "Yolanda B."

Apparently someone at the publishing house thought that Chris had solicited a testimonial from his own wife. In an attempt to disguise things, Yolanda Blake was mysteriously changed to Yolanda B.

For those of us who knew both Chris and Yolanda B., the moment was priceless.

Speaking of Chris Blake . . . when we both taught at Union College, he and our department chair, George Gibson, had an ongoing game each morning in which they would greet one another by twirling their hand ceremoniously and bowing as low as possible to the ground.

One morning as he got out of his car, George saw Chris's car coming down the road. Seizing the opportunity, George rushed to the side of the road, twirled his hand, and bowed.

Finally, George looked up to see Chris's reaction. Instead, he saw a middle-aged woman with a confused expression on her face.

Again, speaking of Chris Blake (man, this guy's a hoot!) . . . Sometimes when Chris arrived at work after I did, he thought it was funny to park his car only inches from my driver's side door, making it impossible for me to get in. Instead, I had to crawl across my passenger seat.

One day I got an idea. Just before lunch break my colleague Mark Robison and I rushed out to the parking lot and were delighted to find empty parking spaces on either side of Chris's hatchback. We pulled our cars in tightly on both sides, then climbed out and hid in the bushes.

A few minutes later we saw Chris striding toward the parking lot. As he got closer, he slowed his pace, then stopped altogether. Mark and I leaped out of the bushes. "Yeaahhhhh!" we yelled victoriously.

Without missing a beat, Chris smiled wryly and resumed his walk toward his car. Popping open his hatchback, he forced his six-foot-two-inch frame inside, pulled the hatch shut, nodded at us through the back window, crawled/fell over the back seat, simulated his own birth (headfirst) between the front seats, contorted his body into his driver's seat, started the car, and with a satisfied beep, drove away laughing.

Chapter 22

The Face of Home Depot

I'm about as mechanically gifted as a puffin. I don't get many calls from close friends asking me to help them build or fix something. They'll phone me to help them move some object, but not build or fix anything. When my lawn mower breaks, and I'm on the ground staring at the belts and gears, my daughter Ally, who *is* mechanically gifted, will come lie down beside me and say, "Why don't you just turn this, Daddy?"

So it was all the more comical when, a few summers ago, I found myself standing in the contractor tent at the local Home Depot. I hadn't planned to visit the contractor tent. In reality, I had simply gone to Home Depot to buy some 4" x 4" posts that *my friend* told me to buy so that *he* could build a shelter for the pygmy goats I had gotten several weeks earlier to get the kids away from the TV.

I found the posts successfully and checked out at the contractor exit. The cashier smiled. "Did you get your key for the Big Toolbox yet?" she asked.

"What do you mean?"

"They're running a corporate promotion outside in the contractor tent," she said. "If your key opens the Big Toolbox, you win."

"Oh," I said, as she handed me a key. She must have thought I was a contractor.

I wheeled my cart outside and suddenly found myself in a line of burly contractors, both male and female, waiting to try to open the Big Toolbox. One by one they inserted their key into the padlock, turned the key unsuccessfully, and either sighed or swore.

The contest had been going all day, which meant that lots of people had tried and failed to open the Big Toolbox. My expectations couldn't have been lower as I reached the front of the line and inserted my key.

Click. To my astonishment, *the padlock popped open.* "Oh, crud," the woman behind me said. (She used another word.)

Suddenly a tall man from Home Depot Corporate rushed over with a microphone. "You opened it?" he said excitedly.

I shrugged almost apologetically.

"OK!" he said into the microphone. "Folks, let me have your attention. We've got our big winner. What's your name, sir?"

"Andy Nash," I said into the microphone.

"Great," he said. "And what's your company's name?"

I paused. "The Front Porch," I said. (I was running a publishing company with that name.)

The crowd cheered. Then the Home Depot big shots hustled me outside to have my picture taken with two beautiful Home Depot models in front of the official Home Depot race car. (I was the only thing in the photo that wasn't orange.) The picture would become part of Home Depot publicity materials, making me, in a sense, the face of Home Depot.

After being presented with my prize, I quietly pushed my cart across the parking lot to my minivan. As I drove away, I had a feeling that I'd never felt before. For once in my life, I knew how it felt to be mechanically gifted. After all, I'd opened the toolbox when no one else could!

We can probably all think of times we wish we could suddenly be equipped with an ability that we don't have. How often do we long to be like someone else—to be someone we're not? The irony is, those gifted people we esteem so much? They undoubtedly admire someone else too.

At times God may dramatically give us new gifts and abilities. But for the most part, He simply calls us to be the people He created us to be: bearing the fruits of the Spirit in our own unique way. Choosing to be satisfied with the way He has made us is a lot like inserting a key into a Big Toolbox. Something just clicks.

Chapter 23

Church

In our hearts we know how Jesus would do church. It wouldn't look much like the slick, starched examples on Sunday morning television. And truth be told, it wouldn't look like most of our congregations, either.

I once read a story by a young Colorado pastor, Byard Parks.

"Last week," Byard wrote, "I turned 30—and what a fantastic celebration my friends threw! We went to downtown Colorado Springs and set up a birthday party and invited the homeless and poor. My church family set up grills and served hamburgers with all the fixings, baked potatoes, and birthday cupcakes. More than 125 people came through line. Lots of runaway teenagers, middle-aged homeless men, and even some Hells Angels. As the 'birthday boy,' it was great to have all these tattooed arms outstretched to me in congratulations and smiles from pierced faces who hadn't had 'home-cooked' food in a long time.

"I sat and visited with one young man, Jeremy, who had a Mohawk, pierced eyebrows, and a hankering to talk. He had a scowl like the visit of a demon, and I soon found out he had just bought a gun to murder his father. Recently he had discovered that his father had molested his 12-year-old sister. A couple other runaway teens came over to join us at our picnic table. It seems tattoo dragons and satanic symbol chains don't dampen one's appreciation for food! Just as these newcomers stuffed their mouths with hamburgers, I said, 'I am going to pray here for Jeremy. He's got a lot of rough stuff going on at home. If you boys want to bow your heads, you're welcome to.'

"You've never seen such humble looks! These teens folded their hands like angels, one of them removing his baseball cap, revealing a huge tattoo of a snake coiled on his shaved head. I learned that for lives in pain, prayer is always welcome. Hamburgers can wait when the Bread of Life is being served."

Surprise Party

Byard's birthday party in Colorado reminded me of another one in Hawaii. In his book *The Kingdom of God Is a Party* Tony Campolo tells the now-classic story of a jet-lagged night in Honolulu.

At 3:30 a.m. in a diner Campolo overhears some prostitutes chatting in the next booth. One of them, Agnes, mentions that the next day is her birthday.

"So what do you want, Agnes?" her friend replies sharply. "A birthday party?"

"No," says Agnes. "I was just telling you, that's all. I've never had a birthday party."

After the women leave, Campolo hatches a plan with Harry, the diner's cook, to throw a surprise party for Agnes. The word quietly spreads, and the next night at 3:30 a.m., Campolo, Harry, and a platoon of prostitutes crouch inside the freshly decorated diner as Agnes walks in.

"Happy birthday!" they shout wildly.

At first Agnes can only stare. Then she begins to cry. And when her first-ever birthday cake is revealed, she won't let anyone eat it. "I want to take it home," she says.

During the party Harry learns that Campolo is a minister. "Minister!" he says disgustedly. "What kind of church do you belong to?"

"I belong to a church," Campolo replies, "that throws birthday parties for whores at 3:30 in the morning."

"No, you don't," Harry says. "There's no church like that. If there were, I'd join it."

In our hearts we know how Jesus would do church.

Part 3

Being Adventist

Chapter 24

Justification for Adventists: Just a Reminder

It's only when we understand grace that the Spirit of grace can do His most powerful work in our lives.

Going to church on Saturday does not save you. Neither does eating vegetarian, or even vegan. Nor will refraining from alcohol, tobacco, pot, meth, and heroine gain you salvation. You cannot merit yourself before God.

The amount of time you spend communing with God does not determine your salvation. Nor will the amount of time you spend playing video games or watching television or surfing Web sites you shouldn't be looking at. They can mess up the quality of your life, but they don't determine your salvation.

The bitterness you might feel toward another person right now, or the pain that you've recently caused a friend or family member—these don't settle your salvation. If you're jealous of someone and you take secret pleasure when something goes wrong for them—it, too, doesn't fix your salvation.

If you've had an abortion and you deeply, deeply regret it in your heart, it also does not save you or unsave you. And if you don't really regret the abortion at all, it is not that factor that determines salvation. Such experiences are painful enough without having to lie in bed worrying that somehow you've lost your salvation.

Not sinning doesn't save you, and sinning doesn't keep you from being saved. Nor do any of these automatically cause the loss of salvation: not keeping your body pure, not studying your Bible, not praying, not avoiding drugs, not eating right, not resting on the Sabbath.

The only rest that matters to your salvation is resting in the all-sufficient doing of Jesus Christ. The only work that matters is His. You can't improve on it. If you try to merit yourself before God, then you're making the dangerous mistake of attempting to save yourself, which you cannot do.

Some people say that this is cheap grace. It *is* cheap. It's free. "But now a righteousness from God, apart from law, has been made known, to which the Law and the Prophets testify. This righteousness from God comes through faith in Jesus Christ to all who believe. There is no difference, for all have sinned and fall short of the glory of God, and are justified freely by his grace through the redemption that came through Christ Jesus" (Rom. 3:21-24).

There's nothing you have to strive for in the economy of grace. Grace is what sets apart our faith from all the other religions of the world. Every other religious system operates somehow on works—what you do. Christianity is predicated on what Christ has done for you. Accepting His work—acknowledging that you don't have to save yourself and that you can't save yourself—is the only work we do.

It's true that accepting the work of Christ will make a dramatic difference—that the Spirit of Christ will enter your life and *change* it.

It's true that He who began a good work in you will be faithful to complete it. (It's He who completes it, not you.)

It's true that the New Testament spends comparatively little time on how to be saved and much more time on living like citizens of the kingdom.

It's true that our behavior has everything to do with living the abundant life in Christ.

But let's be clear. For our salvation, it happens outside of us. It is Christ's work, not our own. "For it is by grace you have been saved, through faith—and this is not from yourselves, it is the gift of God—not by works, so that no one can boast" (Eph. 2:8, 9).

Only when we understand grace can the Spirit of grace do His most important work in our lives.

Chapter 25

Your Mistakes . . . and Grace

Have you ever found yourself in a royal mess? Maybe you made a decision in life, or a series of them, that completely got you off track. Later you realized that you should have gone *that* way, but instead you went *this* way.

A couple years ago I was driving to the beach in South Carolina with a friend, Alex Bryan. Our wives and kids had left about an hour before us, so Alex and I were trying to make up time. We stopped for gas and something to eat and then got back on the interstate. About 30 minutes later Alex suddenly lurched forward and yelled, "We're going the wrong way!" Sure enough, we were heading west, not east. That meant that we'd lost an hour of time and that the girls were going to be splashing at the beach without us that evening.

It was quiet in the car for the next hour as Alex and I saw the same things out the window for the second time: same signs, same landmarks, same herd of cows.

Wrong Place, Wrong Time

Like sheep (or cows) that have gone astray—each its own way—we've all wandered down the wrong road in both big and small ways. One of my life regrets, I realized later, was to pursue a graduate degree in the wrong field, English, because the English professor I'd had in college seemed so happy teaching the subject, and I thought I would be too. But a few weeks in, I had this sinking feeling that I was in the wrong place. The problem wasn't the program; the problem was me—I just wasn't the right fit. I was studying at Andrews University, so I started walking across campus to the seminary and taking all the theology classes I could. That, I realized, was what I really loved: the deep study of Scripture. But it was too late and too expensive for me to change course. I was already on a track that I couldn't turn back from.

How many of us wish we could go back?

Some of us get into relationships that simply are not healthy, and people around us—who aren't in love and can see straight—tell us that some cold day we're "really going to regret this decision." But we don't listen because we're sure that our true love will change when we get married and have children. "It will be OK, you'll see."

Others of us decide to wander a while on a path of sin—just because we're young and we want to "experience the world" and "sow our wild oats." How harmless can that be? The problem is, our wild oats may keep growing into something that we spend our lives harvesting.

A friend of mine once talked to a middle-aged man whose life was in shambles. The man kept repeating, "Look what that 18-year-old kid did to me. Look what that 18-year-old kid did to me." He was talking about *himself*. Having made some life-altering mistakes when he was young, he was still paying the price for them.

When we realize our lives are supposed to be over *there,* and somehow we've found ourselves over *here,* it can be a lonely feeling.

A Royal Mess

One of the most dire situations in biblical history appears in Esther 3. Even though the Jewish people were now allowed to return to Israel following their captivity, many of them had decided to take their chances in Persia, where King Xerxes reigned. Apparently they thought, *Hey, how bad could it be to hang out here for a while? Daniel seemed to do OK in Babylon. His three friends seemed to get a warm welcome there. Why not experience the world?*

One of the Jews whose family hadn't gone back to Palestine was a man named Mordecai, who had descended from the tribe of Benjamin. Mordecai was the cousin of the beautiful Esther, who had recently been made the new queen of Persia—which meant that she got to see King Xerxes whenever King Xerxes felt like it.

In Esther 3:1-6 we read: "After these events, King Xerxes honored Haman son of Hammedatha, the Agagite, elevating him and giving him a seat of honor higher than that of all the other nobles. All the royal officials at the king's gate knelt down and paid honor to Haman, for the king had commanded this concerning him. But Mordecai would not kneel down or pay him honor.

"Then the royal officials at the king's gate asked Mordecai, 'Why do you disobey the king's command?' Day after day they spoke to him but he refused to comply. Therefore they told Haman about it to see whether Mordecai's behavior would be tolerated, for he had told them he was Jew.

"When Haman saw that Mordecai would not kneel down or pay him honor, he was enraged. Yet having learned who Mordecai's people were, he scorned the idea of killing only Mordecai. Instead Haman looked for a way to destroy all Mordecai's people, the Jews, throughout the whole kingdom of Xerxes."

In verse 1 we find a word pregnant with meaning. The word is Agagite. Haman the Agagite. Later, in verse 10, we see Agagite defined as the "enemy of the Jews." What's behind all this? To get our answer, we need to go way back in time.

Nothing but a Family Thing

About 1,500 years earlier, not far from Persia, God told Abraham and Sarah of the breathtaking plans and promises He had for them and their descendants. They began to be fulfilled when Abraham and Sarah had a son: Isaac. Later Isaac and his wife, Rebekah, had two sons: Jacob and Esau. Esau was born first and was supposed to carry on God's promise. He, not Jacob, should have been the one renamed Israel. It was Esau's sons, not Jacob's, who should have become the tribes of Israel.

But Esau took his long-term calling lightly and was willing to trade it for his immediate appetite: "Forget the future; I'm hungry right now!" By the time Esau had polished off his pot of stew, he had lost his calling to Jacob, who was whistling in the kitchen. It would now be Jacob who would be renamed Israel and would have 12 sons—the tribes of Israel, the children of Israel.

Though Esau and Jacob would someday patch things up (see Gen. 33), Esau's descendants, called the Edomites, wouldn't be quite so gracious to Jacob's descendants, the Israelites. Esau's grandson was named Amalek, and his descendants were called the Amalekites. The Amalekites were a wandering people who boasted that they were the first of all nations—an interesting assertion considering that Esau had lost his place as the firstborn. The Amalekites were slave traders and child sacrificers, and were known for their cruelty, specializing in hit-and-run warfare against the weak. Deuteronomy 25:17-19 records: "Remember what the Amalekites did to you along the way when you came out of Egypt. When you were weary and worn out, they met you on your journey and cut off all who were lagging behind; they had no fear of God. When the Lord your God gives you rest from all the enemies around you in the land he is giving you to possess as an inheritance, you shall blot out the memory of Amalek from under heaven. Do not forget!" Interestingly, we find no reference to the Amalekites outside of Scripture.

The Amalekites appear again in 1 Samuel 15, when Israel has just named its first king—Saul, the son of Kish, from the tribe of Benjamin. The first real test of Saul's kingship is an order to completely destroy the Amalekites and their king, Agag, because of their wickedness. For several hundred years amnesty had been available to groups such as the Amalekites. They had the opportunity to live peaceably in Israel as immigrants or to leave the land, as undoubtedly many did. But under their new king, Agag, the Amalekites had become more and more depraved (some commentators speculate that they were rife with sexually transmitted diseases), and the cup of God's wrath had been filled.

So God commanded King Saul to destroy these descendants of Esau. But instead, Saul used his own judgment and only partially destroyed the Amalekites, sparing King Agag himself and some of the choice livestock. To "partially destroy" is an oxymoron. You can't partially get rid of something. For example, you can't partially give up a bad habit. Either you abandon it or you don't. That was Saul's fatal error. He didn't entirely destroy the problem.

In turn, the prophet Samuel ripped Saul's crown from him and gave it to a simple shepherd boy down the road in Bethlehem, from the tribe of Judah. David would struggle with sin too, but the difference with him was that he didn't act as if he knew better than God. Humbling himself, he repented and kept fighting the fight—a man chasing after God's own heart.

Meanwhile, the remnants of the Amalekite people burned with hate toward Israel. Commentators suggest that their descendants now went by the name of their king Agag: the Agagites. One of them was Haman.

So it's here in Esther 3 that Haman the Agagite and Mordecai the Jew (from the same tribe of Benjamin as King Saul) find themselves face to face in Persia. We can now better understand why Haman the Agagite was so bent on annihilating the Jews, and why Mordecai the Jew refused to bow to Haman. It was nothing but a family thing.

One mistake—Saul's refusal to obey God—nearly resulted in the annihilation of the Jewish people. Some will protest, "Why was it OK for the Amalekites to be annihilated but not the Jews?" It's a very hard question, but at the end of the day we have to let God be God. That was Saul's mistake: he didn't let God be God. In fact, it was Saul who was attempting to be God.

When the order for the destruction of the Jews went out, God intervened—saving His chosen people. He turned the thirteenth day of the twelfth month from an occasion of death for the Jews into one of life and celebration—now called Purim.

The curious thing about the book of Esther is that it doesn't even mention God.

Without Him in the picture, we might feel as if our lives here on earth are determined by human will or seemingly random events—the roll of the dice (the word Purim means casting of lots—or rolling of dice). But that is precisely why we have the book of Esther: to show the hand of God working behind everything. God's economy has no randomness in it. There's no rolling of the dice. Anytime He wants He can reach His hand into the affairs of our world and intervene.

A Second Chance

Just as God turned the dice of the world into part of His divine plan, He sometimes chooses to intervene directly in the day-to-day events of our lives. At times He heals physically. Other times He intervenes in relationships and career paths. Fifteen years after I realized how much I loved the study of Scripture, the Lord gave me the privilege of being on the pastoral staff of our campus church—working under a new senior pastor, Dave Smith, my old English professor. Both of our lives had taken an unexpected turn.

It's true that some must pay severe consequences for choices they've made. They may do so behind bars, ruining their opportunity to serve as they might wish. But there's so much more than our brief time here on our sin-plagued earth. Another of my former professors, R. Lynn Sauls, tells a story about arriving at a Boston museum with his wife just before closing. It was their only chance to visit this museum—and yet he knew he couldn't possibly see it all. There simply wasn't enough time!

Now in his 70s, Professor Sauls said that that's what life has been like for him. Although he had so much that he wanted to do, life has gone by so quickly, and he just didn't have time. "But," he once told me with a twinkle in his eye, "on the new earth we'll have all the time we need."

Chapter 26

Knowing God's Will:
Is It Supposed to Feel
Like a Scavenger Hunt?

If you believe in a personal God who cares about every aspect of your life, why is it so hard sometimes to figure out what His will for you is? Well, maybe it's not as difficult as we make it. Perhaps it really isn't the scavenger hunt that it feels like.

Let's start with that phrase itself. When you think about knowing God's will for your life, what kind of things immediately come to mind? Your career? Your relationships? Where you should live? While it's important to know His desires about such things, let's first think about other aspects of the divine will.

Do we know God's intent for how we should treat others? Yes, we do. When the light turns green and the car in front of us doesn't move because the driver is texting, we know how we should respond. Scripture tells us to be patient with others, to be loving, even when the first thing the suddenly alerted driver does is look at you in the rearview mirror. (Don't look at me! Just go!)

How about the way we should conduct ourselves on Monday morning? Yes. Scripture tells us: "Whatever you do, work at it with all your heart" (Col. 3:23). The fact that Paul first gave the counsel to slaves should make us sit up and ask ourselves, Am I working at my current job with all my heart—even if I don't really like it?

So we know quite a bit about God's plans for us. We know how we're supposed to treat others, and we should live and work with integrity and honor the Lord in all that we do. Thus we know 99 percent of what God seeks for us.

Often what we *really* mean when we talk about knowing God's will involves finding out His plans for our future—our career, our relationships, exciting things like that. Does God care about these, too? Yes, He is concerned about everything in our lives. So how do we "figure out" His will in those areas?

The Greatest Hits

It's interesting to consider those passages that tend to be popular when we're seeking God's will for our lives. They are the greatest hits—the best sellers. Let's see if we can find a common thread coming through.

Greatest Hit No. 1: "Delight yourself in the Lord and he will give you the desires of your heart. . . . If the Lord delights in a man's way, he makes his steps firm" (Ps. 37:4-23).

Message: Focus on your relationship with the Lord, and release to Him your plans. You don't have to "figure out" God's will for you. If He "delights" in the way you're heading, your steps will be firm. But if they aren't, you should stop or turn around.

Greatest Hit No. 2: "Trust in the Lord with all your heart and lean not on your own understanding; in all your ways acknowledge him, and he will make your paths straight" (Prov. 3:5, 6).

Message: Focus on your relationship with the Lord, and release to Him all your plans. The word "acknowledge" in the original Hebrew means to know someone intimately. The same word appears in Genesis 4:1: "And Adam knew Eve his wife; and she conceived" (KJV).

Greatest Hit No. 3: " 'For I know the plans I have for you,' declares the Lord, 'plans to prosper you and not to harm you, plans to give you hope and a future. Then you will call upon me and come and pray to me, and I will listen to you. You will seek me and find me when you seek with all your heart' " (Jer. 29:11-13).

Message: Focus on your relationship with the Lord, and release to Him all your plans. Accept the reality that His plans may not match yours. Read the early portion of Jeremiah 29 and you'll see God telling His people to stop striving for Jerusalem but instead to settle down and plant gardens in Babylon. In other words, bloom where you're planted.

Greatest Hit No. 4: "Therefore I tell you, do not worry about your life, . . . but seek first his kingdom and his righteousness, and all these things will be given to you as well. Therefore do not worry about tomorrow, for tomorrow will worry about itself. Each day has enough trouble of its own" (Matt. 6:25-34).

Message: Focus on your relationship with the Lord, and release to Him all your plans. The Lord Himself came among humanity to deliver this same counsel. And by His Spirit, He now comes even nearer.

Chapter 27

Bloom Where You're Planted

A few years ago we decided to sell our house. For us, the decision was twofold. First, the cost. Our house—which came with five wonderful acres—was a stretch from the start, a remnant of a period in which I, the giving father, reached as high as I could. I wanted space for our children— space to play and animals to play with. As a trade-off, we wound up with limited space financially and emotionally. It was probably a mistake, this purchase, as much as we enjoyed it. It certainly wasn't the investment I expected it to be.

The other factor was life itself. We noticed our three daughters beginning to move on—from swings and animals to music and school sports. Plus, the house only had one shower—with more and more people lining up for it. So we sold the goats and horses and put out the "For Sale" sign. It was time for a change of seasons.

But after a year—because we live in the United States of America— the house hadn't sold. The market was way down, and we couldn't drop our price any further. *What,* we wondered, *do you do with a former dream home you can't sell?* Finally we decided: Make it your dream home again. The "For Sale" sign still remained out front, but we weren't going to sit there and wait for the future. We were going to live for the present.

That spring we disconnected the television and bought two Cheviot sheep: a pregnant ewe named Lily and a fat ram named Buddy. I had never heard of the breed before.

"Are Cheviots good?" I asked the woman who had placed an ad on Craigslist.

"Yes, Cheviots are really good," she assured me. "They have clean faces, not heavy wool."

Clean faces. Sounded good to me. I said we'd buy them.

After a 90-minute drive, the girls and I arrived in our SUV, with two medium-sized dog cages in the back. When I saw our sheep, I quickly realized that we had a problem. Lily the pregnant ewe might possibly fit in a cage, but Buddy the ram was very, very fat. He looked like a 200-pound seat cover.

"It's OK," the owner assured us. "You can just tie Buddy down in the back."

We entered the sheep pen to greet Buddy and Lily, who stood motionless. I turned to pet some of the lambs scampering about. Just as I leaned down, I felt myself lurch forward. Buddy had rammed me from behind. The girls shrieked with laughter.

"Does he do that often?" I asked the owner.

"Yeah, you have to be careful. I wouldn't turn my back on him."

We loaded/shoved/chinked Buddy and Lily into our SUV and headed home. Every time I looked in the rearview mirror, I saw the three faces of my daughters and one mammoth face of Buddy. *This is going to be interesting,* I thought.

When we got Buddy home, we quickly learned that it didn't matter what part you turned toward him. He rammed us every chance he got. Fortunately, he didn't have horns, or we'd all be lying in a field bleeding to death. But still, it wasn't very pleasant getting thunder-butted all the time. He'd get a certain look in his eye and then back up several steps to get a good run at you. Once Cindy was patting Buddy on the head, which we later learned sheep take as a sign of aggression. Buddy took several steps backward and lowered his big head.

"Don't you dare!" Cindy yelled just as Buddy charged, ramming her in the thigh.

"That hurt!" she said, glaring at me.

We enjoyed inviting friends over so that they too could get rammed by Buddy. For Easter we had a massive egg hunt, and we hid some of the best eggs in the field with Buddy.

No risk, no reward!

Cindy once remarked that Buddy reminded her of Daniel 8:4: "I saw the ram pushing westward, and northward, and southward; and no beasts could stand before him, neither was there any that could deliver out of his hand; but he did according to his will, and magnified himself" (ASV).

I began carrying a staff to comfort me.

Lily, meanwhile, was much more genteel, subdued, and, well, sheepish. Sheep aren't the brightest bulbs, and each morning when we'd walk out to feed them, Lily would stare at us blankly, as if to say, "Have I ever seen anyone before?" A shake of the grain bucket seemed to bring her back.

We spent the first few days trying to get a good underside look at the pregnant Lily to she if she was "bagging up." Finally I grabbed her and flipped her into a seat belt-like position while Cindy and the girls played obstetrician. Each morning we ran out to the field to check on Lily—was today *the* day? But she always just stared blankly, and we began to lose some hope that we'd have a baby lamb to take to the outdoor Easter pageant our church did every year.

Early on the morning of Palm Sunday, Morgan and I crossed the footbridge leading to the field. Standing there in the wet green grass, Lily didn't gaze at us as she usually did. She was too busy tending to the perfect newborn lamb tottering beside her, whiter than white! Morgan screamed, and then I did too. "Baby lamb! Baby lamb!" We ran back across the bridge to the house, where Cindy, Ally, and Summer stumbled out of bed into their clothes and rushed outside with us to see.

What do you do when the seasons won't change? You bloom where you're planted.

Chapter 28

Give Up Your Dreams

Recently I spoke to a group of high school seniors and told them something that they probably didn't expect.

I told them that, at age 18, they were at a time of life when they were probably getting a lot of advice that went something like this:

Follow your heart.

Sacrifice everything for your dreams.

Never, ever, ever, ever, ever, ever, ever, ever, ever give up. (Ever, ever.)

Since they were already receiving plenty of advice for age 18, I was just going to skip that step and tell them what advice I'd give them when they were 28 or 38.

The advice would be this: *Give up your dreams.*

Huh?

I acknowledged that my counsel was a little unusual for high school graduates—perhaps a little uninspiring. How often do you see "Give up your dreams" as a senior class vision statement? Or how often do you find it on a greeting card? "Dear Graduate: Give up your dreams. Love, Grandma."

But I absolutely believe it is one of the most important things we can ever do—give up our dreams.

When I say to give up your dreams, I told the students, I don't mean that you shouldn't still have dreams and desires in your heart. You should. And as you move forward into college and a career, you should work hard at whatever you do.

But you also have to be careful not to clutch too tightly to your own plans and dreams, because they can end up becoming too important to you. They can become a god.

I have a friend who was a gifted writer coming out of college. In fact, all he wanted to do was write a best-selling novel. Writing a novel was his dream, and he woke up and went to bed thinking about it. He traveled throughout Europe doing research for his novel, then lived on a kibbutz in Israel. He was a Jew—a very secular Jew. As he continued working on his novel, he fell in with some Christian friends and began to learn about Yeshua, Jesus, the Messiah. After an incredible series of events, he was baptized in the Jordan River.

But my friend's story wasn't yet complete—in fact, he wasn't truly converted, even after being baptized in the Jordan. He returned to the U.S. and continued working on his novel. One night as he walked the streets of Gainesville, Florida, he kept hearing a voice again and again in his head: *If you want Me, you've got to burn the book. If you want Me, you've got to burn the book.* That book was my friend's most cherished dream, his deepest desire. There was nothing he wanted to clutch onto more. *If you want Me, you've got to burn the book.*

It was as though my friend had known it all along. His life didn't have room for two masters. He went back to his apartment and, using a hot plate his mom had given him to cook on, he set his manuscript on fire. Then he literally watched his dream go up in smoke.

I Want Your Best

This is one of the most spiritual experiences you can ever have—letting go of what you most want to clutch onto—because it means you're deciding to obey the first commandment: "You shall have no other gods before me" (Ex. 20:3).

I invited the students to go back to their rooms that night and read Malachi 1. Malachi 1 is all about giving up what you most want to hold on to. The Jews were supposed to bring their best animals for sacrifice. Instead, they were offering their worst.

God said to them: "When you bring injured, crippled, or diseased animals and offer them as sacrifices, should I accept them from your hands?"

Why did it matter to God what kind of animals people used for sacrifice? Because by giving Him our best, we're putting the most faith in Him. A sacrifice, by definition, is supposed to feel painful to us. It doesn't hurt to surrender our worst. Ask a child to give away a toy they don't play with anymore, and they will do it without much protest. But then ask a child to relinquish their best toy—their favorite doll or car—and see how they react. It's no different as we get older. What do we value most in our life? Are we willing to put that on the altar?

God asks us to release what we want to clutch on to—a sacrifice without defect. Here's the interesting part: When an animal sacrifice was cooked in the fire, a portion of it typically went back to the priest for him to eat. So what the worshipper offered, the worshipper also ate. If you present what's pure, you eat what's pure. But if you offer what's tainted, you eat what's tainted.

The emotions in Malachi weren't all that different from those in Matthew when a bright young man wanted to follow Christ—but wasn't willing to give up what mattered most to him. Jesus said, "You still lack one thing. Sell everything you have and give to the poor, and you will have treasure in heaven. Then come, follow me" (Luke 18:22).

Jesus didn't give this same counsel to every wealthy person He met. But for this young man, money had become too important. It had become a god and was keeping him from the fullness of life in Christ. The man walked away sad—he wasn't willing to give up his best.

It isn't just the bad things that keep our relationship with God from soaring. It can also be the good things: things that become too important to us, things we wake up and go to bed thinking about. They can include careers, dreams, possessions, relationships, and even some of the most honorable things on earth, including service and ministry. All of them can become too obsessive to us.

In my memoir *Paper God* I shared my own experience with this: a personal dream years ago of publishing my own magazine. I took such a massive risk that I was, in effect, sacrificing other areas of my life to pursue this one. Though my dream itself was a good dream, it became too important to me. I grew to despise it, and so did my family.

Stepping out in faith isn't supposed to be exciting—it's supposed to be painful. It means walking *away* from what matters most to us, leaving it on the altar to be refined by the fire of God.

After my friend burned his book, he experienced great peace in His life. Incidentally, God didn't take away his gift for writing. He transformed it. Clifford Goldstein went on to be one of the leading writers in the Adventist Church. But first his gift needed to be refined in the fire: the fat burned up and the blood drained.

Give up your dreams. Entrust to God what you most want to clutch on to. Then watch what happens.

Chapter 29

Your Influence . . . on Your Children's Children's Children

Not long ago I went upstairs to say good night to our three daughters. As I was leaving Ally's room I noticed that she had something pinned to her wall—a purple Minnesota Vikings jersey. Now, there really aren't many good reasons a 13-year-old girl living in Chattanooga, Tennessee, would have a Minnesota Vikings jersey on her wall. Minnesota is a long way away, and the Vikings were terrible right then. It was actually a little embarrassing to have a Vikings jersey.

But actually, Ally *wanted* to have one to wear. And my younger daughters, Morgan and Summer, announced that they did too. Whatever for? For one simple reason: Because I'm their dad. The girls know that I grew up in Minnesota and that I've liked the Vikings since I was a kid. They've heard the story from their grandma about how, when I was in kindergarten, I used only two crayons: purple and yellow. My kindergarten teacher actually sent home a note asking, "Why does Andy color everything purple and yellow?" The girls think that's funny, so they like the purple team too. Just because of me.

I got to thinking about other ways I've influenced the lives of my three girls, who will someday be three women. It's very humbling for a parent to consider such things.

In some ways I feel good about the influence I have on my daughters. I'm honest, I communicate, and I don't have a racist tendency that I'm aware of. Furthermore, I'm affectionate with the girls the way my parents were with my sister and me. And I know that being loving and affectionate with them means they will likely be the same way with their own children—and that they will likely marry a man who's loving and affectionate toward children. Both Cindy and I enjoy the study of Scripture, and it's rewarding to see the same devotion taking root in our daughters' hearts as they begin to grapple with the text and apply it to their lives. Once at church I challenged our members to read their Bible in a month. Later that week I walked past our 7-year-old

Summer's room—and she was lying in bed reading her children's Bible with a clip-on light. I walked over and said, "What are you doing, Summer?" She told me she was reading through the Bible in a month. It about broke my heart when I looked and saw she was on Genesis 2.

But I can think of other areas of life where I wish that I'd been a better influence. Times I've been inattentive to what the girls are trying to tell me or show me. Preoccupied with my own plans to provide a better life when life is right there before my eyes. I have regrets about times I've been impatient and irritable at home—usually stemming from frustration I feel in other areas of life and work. Why should kids have to receive the brunt of a parent's frustrations? Do we want them to think this is normal—to accept it in the people they will marry?

I have regrets about times our family has spent in the murky regions of pop culture—media, music, film. It wasn't necessarily bad stuff, but was it the best use of our time and minds? Or was it just a tranquilizing drug to pass our days—and evenings—on earth?

The influence that parents have over their kids—they pile into our minivans, trusting in wherever we take them, learning from us what's OK and what's not.

Years ago I was at a gas station, and a guy pulled up beside me in a beat-up car. In the back seat were two kids about ages 5 and 7. Blasting out of the car's speakers was some of the most crass rock lyrics I'd ever heard, and I could see the kids' lips moving with the lyrics—clearly they had heard the song many times. Just little kids. Seemingly no chance.

To the Third and Fourth Generation

Perhaps the most startling of the commandments written by the finger of God is the second one—especially the last half: "You shall not make for yourself an idol in the form of anything in heaven above or on the earth beneath or in the waters below. You shall not bow down to them or worship them; for I, the Lord your God, am a jealous God, punishing the children for the sin of the fathers to the third and fourth generation of those who hate me, but showing love to a thousand generations of those who love me and keep my commandments" (Ex. 20:4-6).

The King James Version memorably reads "visiting the iniquity of the fathers upon the children unto the third and fourth generation of them that hate me; and shewing mercy unto thousands of them that love me, and keep my commandments."

What a hard-hitting verse—the iniquity of the fathers affecting the children, grandchildren, and great-grandchildren. What could it possibly mean?

It doesn't indicate that God penalizes someone for the sins of someone else. What it does signify is that the choices that people make have consequences, and often it's the children who suffer them. This rings true because we see it all around us. We know that the way parents treat their children will likely have a direct impact on their children's life. Furthermore, the field of genetics tells us that genes passed down from parents and grandparents can result in certain tendencies or predispositions in a child.

But here's the truly fascinating part: According to the latest science, not only is our behavior shaped by our genes, but our genes get affected by our behavior. In other words, the choices that young people—preparents— are making right now will influence the genetic code of their children and grandchildren.

The Sins of the Grandfathers

On October 30, 2011, *Newsweek* magazine published an article called: "The Sins of the Grandfathers: What happens in Vegas could affect your offspring. How early-life experiences could cause permanent changes in sperm and eggs."

The article, written by Sharon Begley, discusses the powerful effects that the lifestyle choices of future parents have on the genetic code of their descendants. "'The life experiences of grandparents and even great-grandparents,' says molecular biologist Michael Skinner, 'alter their eggs and sperm so indelibly that the change is passed on to their children, grandchildren, and beyond. It's called transgenerational epigenetic inheritance: the phenomenon in which something in the environment alters the health not only of the individual exposed to it but also of that individual's descendants.'"

Scientists discovered this in part by testing lab animals. For example, when they exposed a young animal to a person smoking, or it was malnourished or overfed, this left an imprint on the animal's eggs or sperm—one so "tenacious" that it affected not only its offspring but also its descendants. Researchers traced it all the way to the fourth generation.

In one experiment Australian scientists "fed healthy, svelte, male rats a high-fat diet." As expected, "the rats put on weight and fat, and developed insulin resistance and glucose intolerance—basically type 2 diabetes."

None of that was surprising. "What made the scientists take notice," Begley writes, "was the daughters these rats later sired: although their mothers were of normal weight and ate a healthy diet while pregnant, daughters of the high-fat-diet dads developed insulin resistance and glucose resistance as adults—even though they never ate a high-fat diet themselves." The fathers had no contact with the daughters except through the sperm that created them. In other words, their behavior affected their genes.

Such findings raise the "intriguing possibility that the [human] childhood obesity epidemic is at least in part due to alterations in sperm caused by fathers-to-be eating a high-fat diet." It could explain why obesity in babies has risen 73 percent since 1980. (In other words, the way young men eat before they become fathers has an impact on the babies they will someday have.)

A 2006 study on humans found that if a father had begun smoking before age 11, his sons had a greater body mass index than did sons of men who took up smoking as adults.

But transgenerational effects can also be very positive. "When 15-day-old female mice frolicked for two weeks in an enriched environment, one filled with exercise wheels, novel objects, and other mice for social stimulation, it strengthened the brain mechanism that underlies memory." Such neuronal effects also show up in the mice's offspring—"even when those offspring never lived in an enriched environment, and even though those offspring were not so much as a gleam in their mothers' eyes when they lived in the enriched environment."

In much the same way, if a human grows up in an intellectually enriched environment, their children and grandchildren may reap the rewards genetically. What this means for preparents is that the choices they're making right now will shape the genes that they pass on to their children. So much for the idea that you can safely sow your wild oats in youth. (After I'd shared this research at church, one college guy told me afterward, "I'm going to lose weight, and I'm going to frolic!")

Such groundbreaking research (which affirms the second commandment) should motivate all of us to make better choices for the sake of our children and grandchildren. Those who are older can also make a difference by modeling love and a high standard to those in their lives. These findings should also make us more compassionate toward those around us. Some people carry very heavy burdens—tendencies they didn't choose but still bear. We should be patient with each other, not truly understanding what it's like to walk in another's shoes—and that for some people, to be "good" is much harder than for others.

Still, we must be careful not to go too far here. We are not lab animals or robots. Each of us has free choice, regardless of our genes or circumstances. The miracle of redemption in Christ does not bow its head to the laws of genetics or environment. Some of the most beautiful moments in history are the dramatic transformations of people steeped in sin who suddenly realize that they are not predestined to the sins of the fathers but that they have been born again and adopted by their heavenly Father through faith in His Son—and our Brother—Jesus Christ. "Therefore, if anyone is in Christ, he is a new creation; the old has gone, the new has come!" (2 Cor. 5:17).

Chapter 30

Make the Most of Your Time

When Paul spent three years teaching in the very secular city of Ephesus, he explained that God isn't content with just saving each of us—He also wants us to have the abundant life He intended for us all along. "For I have not hesitated," said Paul, "to proclaim to you the whole will of God" (Acts 20:27).

The whole will of God, theologian John Piper points out, is much more than simply knowing the name of Jesus. Jesus is far more than a word—He's a completely new way of life. And if we want to experience this way of life fully, we will need to make some changes.

An Important Distinction

A believer might pray two different prayers. The first is: "Save me, Lord, in spite of me." Such a prayer is at the very heart of the gospel. No matter how bad or good we might be, we are all sinners, we all fall short, and we all have to be saved outside of ourselves. Our flesh and spirit wage war against each other, and sometimes the flesh wins. But humbly accepting the fact that Jesus gave His life for us is what saves us. He paid the price of sin, which is death. And by accepting His death as our substitute, we have eternal life. "Save me, Lord, in spite of me." We all have to pray this prayer.

The other prayer that Christians might offer is: "Use me, Lord, in spite of me." There's also some level of truth in this prayer, because, as sinners, we will always depend on God to take our meager efforts and bless them. But sometimes what we really mean when we pray "Use me in spite of me" is that we don't want to put in any work. We take the attitude that even though I haven't made much effort, even though I haven't lived the way that I should be living, I want You, God, to bless my efforts anyway. This is kind of like praying, "Help me to run a marathon when I haven't spent any time training"; "Help me to do well on my exam when I haven't spent any time studying"; "Help me to be a marine without basic training."

For God to save us, we don't have to do anything but confess that we need a Savior. But to be used by God to bless others, including our own families, we have to be willing to participate. We have to empty out the garbage and distractions in our lives—to be vessels that God can then refill.

Scripture has a story about Moses that most people don't even know. After God had called him to deliver his people, Moses was returning to Egypt with Zipporah and their newborn son. But then this startling incident happens: "At a lodging place on the way, the Lord met Moses and was about to kill him. But Zipporah took a flint knife, cut off her son's foreskin and touched Moses' feet with it. 'Surely you are a bridegroom of blood to me,' she said. So the Lord let him alone" (Ex. 4:24-26).

Wow! What a change in tone. Wasn't Moses God's chosen vessel to lead the Israelites out of Egypt? If he were dead, then how would God deliver His people?

But God didn't need Moses to accomplish His plans. And He doesn't need us. While God invites everyone to execute His will, He depends on no one—not even the mighty Moses. We can only wonder how many Moseses have forfeited their calling along the way.

Walk in the Fullness of God's Blessings

In his letter to the same Ephesian believers he'd spent three years with, Paul holds up a very high standard for the life of faith. "Be very careful, then, how you live—not as unwise but as wise, making the most of every opportunity" (Eph. 5:15, 16).

The purpose of living right, the apostle explains, is not only to experience joy ourselves but to bring joy to those around you. "Sin is sin," writes Martin Weber, "because it destroys our relationships by ruining our capacity to love and be loved." When we break free from the sin and distractions in our lives, we're better able to love those around us. We're better dads and moms, better brothers and sisters, and better friends and coworkers.

At the church where I've participated the past few years, I've noticed something interesting. If I've prepared well for a sermon but haven't had a good week spiritually, my sermon feels more strained as I deliver it—like hard work. However, if I've had a good week spiritually, then my sermon seems much easier to deliver—*even if I haven't had as much time to prepare as I would like*. Obviously the best combination is to prepare well for a sermon *and* to have a good week spiritually, but the most important thing is to be in communion with God and live right.

The way we identify sin and distractions in our lives is an interesting process. At times we might even have trouble seeing the sin. In Ephesians 1 Paul prays that the "eyes of our hearts" will be enlightened so that we can examine our lives clearly. Some people, he explains in verses 17-19, are so far removed from God that they don't even know what right and wrong are anymore. They're desensitized to evil.

The recipients of Paul's letter, those in Ephesus and beyond, came from a highly desensitized culture. In many ways Ephesus was like a Sodom, a Las Vegas, or an Amsterdam. Especially with regard to sexuality, there really wasn't a sense of right and wrong at all. Clinton Arnold writes in *Romans to Philemon* (volume 3 of *Zondervan Illustrated Bible Backgrounds Commentary*) that "adulterous relationships, men sleeping with their slave girls, incest, prostitution, 'sacred' sexual encounters in the local temples, and homosexuality were all a part of everyday life in that culture"(p. 329). William Barclay adds in *The New Daily Study Bible: The Letters to the Galatians and Ephesians*: "The ancient world regarded sexual immorality so lightly that it was no sin at all. It was the expected thing that a man should have a mistress. ... The great temples were staffed by hundreds of priestesses who were sacred prostitutes, and whose earnings went to the upkeep of the temple" (p. 186).

"It has been said, and with much truth," Barclay observes in *The New Daily Study Bible: The Letters to Timothy, Titus, and Philemon* "that the only totally new virtue which Christianity brought into this world was chastity" (p. 85).

While we might be more sensitized to sexual sin in society today, we can be so desensitized to other things that we don't even stop to think about them. Because so many other Christians are watching certain TV programs, we figure it must be OK. When so many other Christians, even whole churches, are enjoying all the Super Bowl commercials, it must be acceptable. And when so many other Christians are illegally downloading music, then it must be permissible.

The other issue is the way we spend our time. An activity might be OK, but is it really worth our time? Is it keeping us from something better? I've had two experiences that have opened my eyes to some things.

One year, in January, I followed a friend's practice of reading through the Bible in a month. I was amazed at the difference it made on my mind. To spend every available minute in study was a transforming experience. Throughout the day, rather than thinking about earthly things, my mind was meditating on what I'd been reading. It changed my life.

I had a similar experience when my daughters and I traveled to Israel.

I said to them, "OK, for the next 12 days we're only going to focus on Israel and the Bible. Nothing else." Without media and other distractions in our lives, it was amazing how calm and focused we were by the end of the trip. When I got back, I couldn't believe how I viewed people. Instead of the usual surface ways, I felt a true concern for their spirituality. If you've taken a mission trip, you will know how it feels to have your whole perspective change.

Evaluating Your Choices

A clear perspective can help us identify what areas of our lives we might need to address. Here are two questions I've found helpful.

First: How do you feel about an activity after it's over? Not during, but after. We have to be honest and acknowledge that many things can be pleasurable for a time, but it doesn't last. As the woman at the well said to Jesus: "Please give me living water so I don't have to keep coming back here to draw water."

The second question is: How do you feel when you see others doing a comparable activity? I grew up watching a lot of sports. I have great memories enjoying the games with my dad. It was a special time together. Through the years I've regularly read the sports news about my favorite teams, as though they couldn't function without my checking in. But I've felt increasingly convicted that it just isn't worth my time. When I see other guys addicted to their own favorite teams, I don't feel impressed. A few years ago I stopped playing fantasy football with my friends because it just consumed too much of my time and thoughts. Also, I've cut down on how much sports I watch on TV, though I do enjoy watching a football game on Sundays with my daughters.

Admittedly, I still struggle to find the right balance with leisure. An old church tradition recounts that when the disciple John was an elder in Ephesus, he had a hobby of raising pigeons. Once another elder was returning from a hunting trip when he saw John playing with his pigeons. The hunter scolded John for being frivolous with his time.

Looking at the hunter's bow, John remarked that the string was loose.

"Yes," said the hunter. "I always loosen the string of my bow when it's not in use. If it stayed tight, it would lose it resilience and fail me in the hunt."

"And I," replied John, "am now relaxing the bow of my mind so that I may be better able to shoot the arrows of divine truth."

Of course, it was John and the other disciples whom Jesus often called to "come away and rest a while."

"The First Step in Renewal Is Demolition"

While we seek to find rest and balance in our lives, we can all think of areas in which we simply need to break free. A prominent Christian pastor says, "The first step in spiritual renewal is demolition."

In the Christian high school I attended, often a Week of Prayer would end with many students making the decision to throw out (or take a hammer to) their CDs. Though some students made fun of such decisions (especially when a student regressed), I believe it was still a deeply spiritual act.

A few years ago in an airport bookstore I saw a business management book titled *The One Thing You Need to Know*. The title intrigued me even though I didn't want to buy the book. So I stood in the bookstore flipping through the 400-page book, trying to find the one thing I needed to know! Finally, about two thirds of the way through the volume, I found it. The one thing I needed to know was: "Identify what you hate—and get rid of it."

While this was management advice, it's certainly true of spiritual life as well. What's one thing that you hate? Get rid of it! Do it for the people around you.

Be Imitators

Paul also said, in Ephesians 5:1, that we should also be "imitators" of those who are living the life of faith. In other words, we should surround ourselves with people who are positive influences. Truly, by beholding, we become changed.

Dennis Hensley tells how in the 1980 Winter Olympics one speed skater, Eric Heiden, was so fast that everyone else knew they had no way of beating him. Heiden entered five races, and everyone realized that if he was on his game, they had no chance of beating him. Sure enough, Heiden easily won every race.

But something interesting happened in each of those five races. The silver and bronze medalists achieved their personal best times. By associating themselves with the best, they skated faster than they'd ever done before. It became known as the Heiden effect.

It's the same, writes Hensley, with Jesus Christ. By imitating the life of Christ and the lives of His followers, it raises our game. It makes us better and changes our identity. Surround yourself with Christ-filled people, and you will become transformed.

Make the most of your time. Don't wait until you have none left. "Let us throw off everything that hinders and the sin that so easily entangles, and let us run with perseverance the race marked out for us" (Heb. 12:1).

Chapter 31

I Can Do All Things?

"I can do all things through Christ who strengthens me" (Phil. 4:13, KJV).

This past winter I've had the privilege of coaching the sixth-grade girls' basketball team at our local Adventist school. The Lady Rapids didn't have a coach, and my daughter Morgan was on the team. How could I pass up the opportunity?

From the start, I've loved coaching the 11 girls. They have terrific attitudes and work hard at learning their positions. But we faced some challenges. First, we were a brand-new sixth-grade program, and we would be playing experienced teams. Second, four of our tallest sixth graders had moved up to the seventh grade team (which didn't have enough players). It was important for us to have realistic expectations.

Before our first practice, I sat the girls down and talked to them about what must be the most popular Bible verse for Christian athletes, Philippians 4:13: "I can do all things through Christ who strengthens me" (KJV). From football player Tim Tebow to one-armed surfer Bethany Hamilton (from the movie *Soul Surfer*), it seems as if nearly every Christian athlete finds inspiration in the verse.

"Do you think," I asked, "that being able to do all things through Christ means that you could go dunk the ball right now?" The girls smiled and shook their heads no.

I told them what this verse actually means: "I can *handle* all things through Christ who strengthens me." Philippians 4:13 teaches us that we can be content in any situation—whether we're winning or losing—because we know Christ. When Paul composed the words "I can do all things through Christ who strengthens me," he was writing from a prison cell.

Then I explained that we couldn't control how high we could jump or how many games we would win, but we could determine how we handled our circumstances. We could choose to carry ourselves with dignity and to show respect for our opponents—whether we won or lost.

We lost our first game 34 to 0.

Never in my wildest dreams did I think we'd be behind by such a wide margin—that we wouldn't score a single point! Our shots rolled around the rim but just wouldn't drop. The team we played, a group of surprisingly tall homeschoolers called the Chattanooga Patriots, had several seventh graders and had been practicing together for a year. We'd been together for a week. Still, it was a traumatic experience for our team, and by the fourth quarter, I couldn't help feeling the gaze of our disappointed home crowd.

That night I barely slept. *Thirty-four to zero?* I wondered if the girls would lose confidence in themselves and in me.

The next day they showed up for practice, positive and ready to go. Our assistant coaches and I helped them with their aggressiveness, explaining that it was possible to be aggressive and content at the same time!

Our second game was scheduled for a month later . . . against the Chattanooga Patriots, the same team! When I first told the girls, their expressions said: Do we really have to go through that again? But they dug in and worked all the harder. During Christmas break, several of the girls—and their families—came out for optional practices. We all had the same look in our eyes: *If we could just score next time!*

The day of the game the players looked tense during warm-ups, so I took them to a separate room to relax their minds. We talked through our anxieties, and then I prayed out loud for each girl, thanking God for the gifts He's given them. Most of all, we prayed that we would handle all things gracefully—through Christ who strengthens us.

Refreshed, the girls ran back to the court and played their hearts out. We lost the game, but scored seven points, a big step forward. You should have heard the wild cheers from the stands when we scored our first basket—a silky smooth jumpshot from 12 feet away.

On those days you feel as if you're losing 34 to 0, remember the Lady Rapids: Calle, Drielly, Emily, Kelly, Megan, Morgan, Olivia, Sarah, Shadai, Shelby, and Sofe. Like them, you can handle all things through Christ who strengthens you.

Chapter 32

Margin:
What Would You Do
With Spaciousness in Your Life?

When Jesus was on earth, He told us not to worry about tomorrow—what we'll eat and drink, what we'll wear, how we'll pay our bills, how we'll have enough time to get everything done.

But what happens when we place ourselves in situations in which we can't help wondering about such things? Perhaps Jesus' admonition not to worry also means to be wise and cautious with the things of earth so that our minds do not get constantly filled with anxiety about them—so that they don't become too important to us.

A while back a friend of mine, Tim Cross, told me about a book called *Margin* by a Christian doctor, Richard A. Swenson. The book is all about having spaciousness in our lives and finances so that when the unexpected happens we're not completely stressed out.

Dr. Swenson terms this space "margin." Here's what he has to say about the difference between a life with margin and one without it.

"The conditions of modern-day living devour margin . . . ," he writes. "Marginless is being thirty minutes late to the doctor's office because you were twenty minutes late getting out of the bank because you were ten minutes late dropping the kids off at school because the car ran out of gas two blocks from the gas station—and you forgot your wallet. Margin, on the other hand, is having breath left at the top of the staircase, money left at the end of the month, and sanity left at the end of adolescence.

"Marginless is the baby crying and the phone ringing at the same time; margin is Grandma taking the baby for the afternoon. Marginless is being asked to carry a load five pounds heavier than you can lift; margin is a friend to carry half the burden. Marginless is not having time to finish the book you're reading on stress; margin is having the time to read it twice.

"Marginless is fatigue; margin is energy. Marginless is red ink; margin is black ink. Marginless is hurry; margin is calm. Marginless is anxiety;

margin is security. . . . Marginless is the disease of the new millennium; margin is its cure" (p. 13).

May I add a few more? Marginless is taking too many college courses to be able to do well in any of them; margin is taking a course load you can handle. Marginless is hoping that your car won't break down anytime over the next three years because to pay for it you'll have to use the credit card that you're already trying to pay down. Margin is having cash set aside with the expectation that your car will need repairs.

Marginless is heroically working a stressful 60-hour week so that you can someday buy that big boat for your family to enjoy. Margin is working a reasonable week, spending more time with your family all year, and renting a boat for a special weekend. (Or making friends with someone who has a boat.)

Cutting Back

The doctor who wrote this book practices what he preaches. Back in 1982, when he had a very stressful medical practice, he cut back his workweek to just three days. He said it wasn't an easy thing to do. It meant giving up a big income and lifestyle and dealing with the pressure put on physicians to carry heavy loads. But he says he has never regretted it.

Now, a lot of us *wish* we could have a three-day workweek. But the issue isn't necessarily just the number of hours or days we work. A lot of times it's the type of work we do, and the levels of mental and emotional stress associated with it. Dr. Swenson writes: "A person can work 12 hours a day, six days a week for an entire life at physical labor and suffer no ill effects— as long as that person has *decision control* over the work schedule. Actually such hard physical labor would usually have salutary health benefits. But if the strain is *mental* and a person is constantly being frustrated, the negative healthy effects can be catastrophic. . . . In one study that compared physical exertion with mental exertion, a patient was first given a cardiac treadmill exam. Despite vigorous physical exercise, the patient's cardiovascular status remained normal throughout. He then was asked to (stand still and) subtract seven from 777 serially for 3.5 minutes. His blood pressure went up forty points."

The book explains that no one talked much about stress prior to the 1950s. But since that decade we've been increasingly inundated with not only mentally taxing work but a bombardment of noise from our culture and media. Our minds and bodies weren't designed to handle such a frantic pace. Rather, God created us to move sedately at a camel's pace. The Lord intended us to follow the natural cycle of the day: working with the sunlight and then resting in the evening shadows. Jesus Himself modeled such a schedule: "Each day Jesus was teaching at the temple, and each evening he went out to spend the night on the hill called the Mount of Olives" (Luke 21:37). But with the invention of electricity, our workdays now spread into the evening.

No Space

In the wired-up culture in which we live, we may not even realize the pressure we feel to be doing multiple things at the same time. It's hard for us to slow down and allow spaciousness in our lives. Once when I was speaking at church, I asked the congregation, "How many of you have used your phone or other gadget since the start of our worship service today—either to text, talk, or surf?" Of the approximately 300 congregants, about 100 of them raised their hands—many of them students.

I didn't ask that question to condemn anyone. I've used my iPhone during church too. And as someone who works with students, I've actually come to see that doing several things at once isn't necessarily the sign of blatant disrespect it used to be. It's often just the way we're conditioned; we've become accustomed to filling any possible gaps with busyness.

I once heard a comment on sports radio about dads using their smartphones and other gadgets while standing in line with their kids at Disney World. Now it's true, the lines at Disney can sometimes last an hour or two, and from a strictly practical standpoint, what's the big deal with getting a little work done while waiting to ride Space Mountain? It's just being efficient, right? When it's time to get on the ride itself, then you can enjoy the Disney experience with your kids.

But that misses the point. Standing in line with your kids *is* the Disney experience. Strangely, I can remember waiting with my parents and sister at Disney World even more vividly than I remember the rides themselves. We'd talk and laugh as we worked through the labyrinth of railings and saw the same sweaty faces again and again. Sometimes I'd stop for about 30 seconds to let space develop ahead of me, which was highly annoying to my sister, whom I blocked with my arm. Then I'd run ahead, savoring all the ground I was covering. Though the ride was the thing, the anticipation with my family was also the thing.

But when we attempt to fill any possible space, we lose the breathing room we're supposed to enjoy with each other. Recently I saw a magazine article title: "Mommy, Stop Texting and Talk to Me."

I think many of us actually like it when we find ourselves forced to have space in our lives—when we go camping without the gadgets or when we live in a place without the hectic schedules and distractions. In terms of quality of life, one of the best years of my life was the one I spent volunteering in Thailand, where we didn't have television, computers, or an excessive workload. I read a lot of books that year, and talked a lot with the people I worked with. In the evenings after class we sat out at the night market eating rice and noodles with our students well into the night.

Admittedly, as an introvert I sometimes felt worn out by the many broken-English conversations I found myself in. Once I was walking on the sidewalk when a young Thai man rushed up to me, eager to practice his English.

"What's my name?" he asked, obviously confused.

I smiled sympathetically. "Your name is Andy," I replied.

"Yes, yes," the man said.

"It's a pleasure to meet me," I added.

The Happiest Place on Earth

A few years ago an ecological group called the New Economics Foundation decided they were going to try to find out what was the happiest place on earth. They set up what they called a "happy planet index" that tried to measure what people put into a place (the resources) versus what they get out.

Out of 178 nations surveyed, they determined the happiest place on earth to be the small Pacific island nation of Vanuatu. Vanuatu was followed by Colombia, Costa Rica, Dominica, and Panama. The United States, in contrast, ranked 150. In fact, none of the G-8 industrialized nations made the top 50.

Prior to this study, the island of Vanuatu was known primarily for inventing bungee jumping. (They use vines, not elastic ropes.) But the happy planet index cited other reasons for happiness, such as the moderate pace of life. In Vanuatu, people do things in the time they naturally take, and they have great respect for the land they live on. Vanuatu has beautiful coastlines and rain forests. It also has no income tax.

Here's the interesting part. Vanuatu actually has high unemployment rates and poverty. A developing county, its economy is ranked 207 out of

233. But as one expert noted: "If you don't have money in Vanuatu you can still live happily. . . . You can grow everything you need to eat. If people have an opportunity to make money, they will take it, but it is not their ultimate aim."

I did a little more research and found that Vanuatu is a largely Christian nation, with a sizable number of Seventh-day Adventists. The national motto of Vanuatu is "In God We Stand," and the national anthem is called "Yumi, Yumi, Yumi," which means "We, We, We."

Obviously, we don't have to live in Vanuatu to be happy. The happiest people in the world, wherever they might live, are those who have a living, breathing relationship with Jesus Christ—and who follow His teachings. Jesus said, "I have come that they might have life, and have it to the full" (John 10:10).

In the book of Matthew, shortly after Jesus told us not to worry about tomorrow He gave the parable of the wise and foolish builders. As Jesus related it, He was standing beside the Sea of Galilee, and people would have understood what He was talking about. During the dry season the sand on the shore felt hard as rock, so it would have been tempting to build a house on the sand. But when the rainy season hit, that sand easily washed away. The wise builder dug down through the sand to the rock foundation to build his house (Matt. 7:24-29).

Which of the two men in this parable is more worried about a storm? The one who built his house on the sand. He *hopes* that there won't be a storm, but he's worried there might be one.

The man who constructed his house on a firm foundation has no need to worry. He is prepared for whatever might happen.

Making Space

The issue with having margin in our lives isn't about the size of one's house. We should be glad that some people have large houses so that the rest of us can have Christmas parties in them. Rather, the important thing is to have space in our lives and budgets so that we're prepared for the unexpected.

In his book *Blinks* Malcolm Gladwell tells about the owner of a security firm in Los Angeles who says that, for a bodyguard, the central facet in protecting someone is the amount of "white space," the distance between the target and any potential assailant. The more white space there is, the more time the bodyguard has to react. And the more time the bodyguard has, the better their ability to read the mind of any potential assailant.

In 1981 when John Hinckley shot President Ronald Reagan, there was no white space. "The Secret Service agent became aware of him [Hinckley] only when he started firing. From the first instance when Reagan's bodyguards realized that an attack was under way . . . to the point when no further harm was done was 1.8 seconds" (p. 46). It all happened in 1.8 seconds. Now, the Reagan attack involved heroic reactions by several people. Nonetheless, every round was still discharged by Hinckley. In other words, those reactions didn't make one single difference, because he was too close. Not enough white space existed between the attacker and the target.

In the same way, without white space in our lives we become vulnerable and very stressed by the unexpected. We simply don't have opportunity to respond.

A few years ago a friend of mine I'll call Tom was telling me how much pressure he used to feel to keep up with other families: to have a lucrative job and all the toys. For many years he strived to attain such a level of living and eventually took a job in which he traveled most of the week. Finally, he just decided, "No, I'm going to let go of this stress and just be me." He took a modest-paying job at a mobile phone store, which he enjoyed. His family bought a small house, his wife homeschooled, and he was home each day by 4:30 without bringing with him much stress from work. Tom was a new person, and his family was a new family.

We each have our own personal decisions to make. And sometimes they aren't easy. Having space in your life might mean saying no even to good things. And having space in your budget might mean settling for a house or lifestyle that humbles you, but humility is also part of the kingdom of God that Jesus told us to seek first.

The subtitle of this chapter is "What Would You Do With Spaciousness in Your Life?" In a way, it was a trick question. The answer is: nothing. If you can achieve spaciousness in your life, protect it. Preserve it. Do whatever you have to do to put your earthly needs at rest so you can devote your mind to seeking the kingdom of God.

"In repentance and rest is your salvation, in quietness and trust is your strength" (Isa. 30:15).

Chapter 33

Steve Jobs and Abandonment

For the past 50 years we had a true genius in our midst—a modern-day Solomon. Apple founder and CEO Steve Jobs gave the people of earth one breathtaking product after another: the Apple II, the Mac, the iPod, the iPhone, the iPad. He once told *BusinessWeek*, "A lot of times, people don't know what they want until you show it to them."

Jobs gave us not only great technology, but great design. He even intended the experience of opening the sleek iPhone box to be pleasurable. During the hospitalization for the cancer that ultimately took his life, wrote his biographer, Walter Isaacson, he refused to wear the mask the doctor put over his face because he said it was badly designed. He ordered the hospital staff to bring five different mask designs—he would pick the one he liked.

While simultaneously inspiring and exacerbating his employees, Jobs knew the importance of getting them out of their silos. When he built a large new office building, he installed only two restrooms so that they would cross paths. Only when a pregnant staff member complained about the 10-minute walk to the restroom did he have more put in.

As gifted as Jobs was, he also was a deeply troubled person full of contradictions. Although he didn't want a reserved parking space, he would park in those reserved for those with disabilities. He tore people to shreds for their ideas—but often came back the next week and acted as though their ideas were his own.

Stung by Abandonment

Those closest to Jobs said that much of his anger and complexity traced back to his abandonment by his birth parents, which deeply stung him.

"The key question about Steve," a friend commented, "is why he can't control himself at times from being so reflexively cruel and harmful to some people. That goes back to being abandoned at birth. The real underlying problem was the theme of abandonment in Steve's life" (*Steve Jobs*, p. 5).

Another friend added, "I think his desire for complete control of whatever he makes derives directly from his personality and the fact that he was abandoned at birth. He wants to control his environment, and he sees the product as an extension of himself" (*ibid.*, p. 4).

Jobs' former girlfriend said that he was "full of broken glass" (*ibid.*, p. 5). Ironically, Jobs left his girlfriend and the daughter born to them out of wedlock at the exact same age as his biological father did him. Later in life Jobs worked to restore his relationship with his daughter.

It was, in a sense, because of abandonment that Jobs, in his teens, rejected Christianity. Coming across a *Life* magazine cover of two starving children, he took the magazine to church and confronted the pastor. "If I raise my finger," Jobs asked, "will God know which one I'm going to raise even before I do it?"

"Yes, God knows everything," the minister replied.

Jobs pulled out the *Life* cover and asked, "Well, does God know about this and what's going to happen to those children?"

"Steve, I know you don't understand, but yes, God knows about that." Jobs never went back to church.

Years later he said: "The juice goes out of Christianity when it becomes too based on faith rather than on living like Jesus or seeing the world as Jesus saw it" (*ibid.*, pp. 14, 15). Buried even in this statement is Jobs' longing for a world in which everyone gets seen and valued.

Before his death in the fall of 2011, Jobs told his biographer, "I'm about 50-50 on believing in God. For most of my life, I've felt that there must be more to our existence than meets the eye. . . . But on the other hand, perhaps it's like an on-off switch. *Click!* And you're gone. Maybe that's why I never liked to put on-off switches on Apple devices" (*ibid.*, p. 571).

Our Primal Desire

Beneath the brilliance and eloquence of Steve Jobs, we can see a little boy questioning why anyone would abandon him and then coming up with ways to make himself invaluable. Years ago I interviewed another modern-day genius, storyteller Garrison Keillor, who had written about his father being gone for long periods when he was a boy. When I asked Keillor about it, he brushed it aside—even crediting kids' desire to get a parent's attention as the impetus for creativity and independence. But Keillor has also developed a reputation for being difficult to understand fully.

I think we underestimate the impact of abandonment on our core being. When I've talked with my college students about death and divorce, nearly all of them say they'd rather lose a parent to death than to divorce. It included one student whose dad had died earlier that year.

I can personally trace my greatest pain to either an experience of abandonment—a best friend moving on, another best friend leaving me out of something—or a fear of abandonment. It fills me with hurt, which I cover with either anger or detachment. (I once heard it expressed that beneath anger is hurt, and beneath hurt is love.) But the following story reminds me that abandonment doesn't have to be the final card played in a relationship. Those cast aside have the opportunity to wash their pain away with the cleansing water of forgiveness.

Friends

When a friend of mine, Matt, was in fifth grade, he found himself torn between two friends: Tim and Doug. Tim was a nice, quiet kid who wanted everyone to be friends. Doug was the de facto leader of the class. Athletic and good looking, he was also controlling. The other boys in the class wanted Doug to like them.

Once during music class Matt was sitting between Tim and Doug. The teacher announced that they would be setting up a new seating chart. "I want all of you to look around you," the teacher said. "If there's anyone that you think you shouldn't sit by, I want you to raise your hand and let me know." The teacher's intent was for students to identify situations that might distract them in class.

But Doug took advantage of the opportunity. Leaning over to Matt, he whispered, "Tell the teacher that you don't want to sit by Tim." At first, Matt hesitated, but Doug kept insisting, "Say that you don't want to sit by Tim."

Finally, bowing to the pressure, Matt raised his hand.

"Yes, Matt?" the teacher said.

"I don't want to sit by Tim."

At that moment Matt looked over at him. Shock and pain filled Tim's face, as if to say, "Why did you do that to me?" Deeply hurt by someone he really liked a lot, Tim ran out of the room.

Things were never the same again between Matt and Tim, and through the years Matt felt a lingering grief for what he'd done. After he graduated from college, Matt returned to his hometown and, pulling into a gas station, saw Tim working there. Tim looked up, recognizing Matt's face. Matt felt nervous. How would Tim respond after all those years?

Racing over to the car, Tim smiled big. "It's so great to see you, Matt!" he said. Matt sighed, the weight of guilt finally leaving his soul.

Abandonment wasn't the final word. Forgiveness was.

Chapter 34

Drifting Away

When I was a senior in college and my sister, Angel, a freshman, our parents called from home in Orlando and said they had planned our spring break. At first Angel and I weren't entirely sure about the development. After all, springs breaks were meant for friends, not families.

"So what are we doing?" I asked.

"Taking a cruise to the Bahamas," they announced.

Suddenly I felt rather family-minded.

It would be our first-ever cruise. The evening before our departure we all went to Target to "gear up," as Dad put it. Snorkels, flippers, shades, sunscreen, underwater cameras—we piled our cart high.

"Can I get a new swimsuit?" Angel asked.

"You bet," Dad replied. It was no time to cut corners.

Early the next afternoon we climbed into our Chevy Astro van and headed down I-95 toward Fort Lauderdale. In just three hours we'd be boarding the Big Red Boat for the vacation of our lives!

"The guy said to be there at 4:30, right?" Mom asked.

"Yup," Dad answered.

At 4:10 we pulled into the parking lot. As the massive cruise ship came into view, Angel and I began to high-five. This was so cool.

Suddenly Dad lurched forward. "That boat's moving, Michelle!"

"Oh, Chuck; it couldn't be."

Dad was right—it *was* moving . . . right out to sea. Slowly, tauntingly, the cruise ship glided away, its ecstatic passengers waving to the shoreline, where one dumbfounded family stood beside their van.

There was no one there to help us. Later, by pay phone, we learned that our booking agent had given us the wrong time. He had told us 4:30 when the actual boarding time was 2:30. There wouldn't be another departure that week. Nor would there be any Nash family cruise. So we just drove the three hours back home, and Dad went to work the next day.

Another Type of Drifting

Hebrews 2:1-3 says: "We must pay more careful attention, therefore, to what we have heard, so that we do not drift away. For if the message spoken by angels was binding, and every violation and disobedience received its just punishment, how shall we escape if we ignore such a great salvation?"

The imagery here is of drifting off course—without realizing it. It can happen spiritually as well as physically. When we don't pay careful attention—meaning to devote ourselves—to what we have learned about our salvation, we run the risk of drifting away without even noticing it.

Of course, when we missed our cruise ship, we weren't the ones at fault—our representative was. Are there times that, spiritually, we depend on others to pay careful attention—and when they don't, we pay the price?

One of the most important things we must do as Christians is to self-feed: to be able to nourish ourselves spiritually, rather than depend on others to do it. Probably the statistic that most troubles me about the Adventist Church is that half of its members do not study the Bible on their own.

How can it be that "people of the Book" aren't even reading the Book themselves? What a toxic, Laodicean state to be in. "So, because you are lukewarm—neither hot nor cold—I am about to spit you out of my mouth. You say, 'I am rich; I have acquired wealth and do not need a thing,' But you do not realize that you are wretched, pitiful, poor, blind and naked. I counsel you to buy from me gold refined in the fire, so you can become rich; and white clothes to wear, so you can cover your shameful nakedness; and salve to put on your eyes, so you can see" (Rev. 3:16-18).

The Lord tells us to buy salve directly from Him, so that we can see clearly—to be responsible for our own salvation and not be dependent on those around us.

Twelve years later my parents tried to take a cruise again—not only with their kids, but also with their grandkids. This time we didn't depend on a travel agent for our journey to sea. We found a cruise ourselves, we booked it ourselves, and we carefully monitored the departure time ourselves. On the day of the cruise, we arrived at the port early—very early. And when the ship sailed, we were actually aboard, relieved and waving farewell to the shoreline.

Chapter 35

Your Life in Six Words

If you could sum up your life in six words, what ones would you choose? In the book *Not Quite What I Was Planning: Six-Word Memoirs by Writers Famous and Obscure*, people described their life in only six words. Here were some of the entries:

"Alive 38 years. Feels like 83."

"Made a mess. Cleaned it up."

"Bad brakes discovered at high speed."

"Sweet wife. Good sons. I'm rich."

"Followed yellow brick road. Disappointment ensued."

"I watched a lot of television."

"Happiest when ignoring huge financial debt."

"Birth, childhood, adolescence, adolescence, adolescence, adolescence."

"I make hamburgers and French fries."

"On the playground alone. 1970, today."

"Happiness is a warm salami sandwich."

"I still make coffee for two."

"I hope to outlive my regrets."

Adventist Collegians and Retirees

At the time this book came out, I was getting ready to speak to two groups of people: Adventist college students and Adventist retirees. I thought it would be interesting to compare how each group would sum up their lives in six words.

Here's what the Adventist college students wrote:

"I shoulda, coulda, woulda, but didn't."

"Never lost. Never lost. Until now."

"Far from home. Closer to God."

"I finally stood up for myself."

"I owe my life to the Ericksons."
"I would have told him yes."

And here's what the Adventist retirees wrote:
"Many big dreams. Only few attained."
"She was attractive, and still is."
"Enjoying my dream. Then Jesus called."
"Been there. Done that. Worn out!"
"Uncle Sam called. Had to go."
"I now realize: Housework never ends."
"Phone call, and it was Christmas."
"Abused in childhood. Blessed in adulthood."
"Irene, wake up. Mama is dying."
"Farm, no rain, depression, no money."
"Japan stole three years of youth."
"Boy, Boy, Boy, Girl, Girl, Done."
"Traded in for a younger model."

It doesn't take long to recognize the deep emotions behind the words. In many respects, the lives of young and old—and for that matter, believers and unbelievers—aren't all that different. Each group experiences joy and pain, celebration and loss, epiphany and confusion. Perhaps the most difficult emotion is regret—the inescapable dread that you've done something terrible, and there's no way you can change it. Regret haunts us like a wreck in the rearview mirror.

And yet, for the believer in Christ, there's one important difference when it comes to life's regrets—a difference that doesn't need six words, but only one:

Forgiven.

Part 4:
Advent

Chapter 36

Longing for a Messiah

In his book *Twelve Years a Slave,* Solomon Northrup describes the living hell of separation between a parent and child as a Black mother watches her son being auctioned to a planter from Baton Rouge. She and her daughter are about to lose forever the boy they love so much.

"All the time the trade was going on, Eliza was crying aloud, and wringing her hands. She besought the man not to buy him, unless he also bought herself and Emily. She promised, in that case, to be the most faithful slave that ever lived. The man answered that he could not afford it, and then Eliza burst into a paroxysm of grief, weeping plaintively. Freeman turned round to her, savagely, with his whip in his uplifted hand, ordering her to stop her noise, or he would flog her. . . . She kept on begging and beseeching the man, most piteously, not to separate the three. Over and over again she told them how she loved her boy. A great many times she repeated her former promises—how very faithful and obedient she would be; how hard she would labor day and night, to the last moment of her life, if he would only buy them all together. But it was of no avail. . . . Randall must go alone. Then Eliza ran to him; embraced him passionately; kissed him again and again; told him to remember her—all the while her tears falling in the boy's face like rain" (pp. 81, 82).

Several years ago I was sitting at an oil change station with my three daughters. As we waited for our car, I noticed an older man watching my girls. He smiled and said, "I had three daughters like them."

"Are they grown up now?" I asked.

"Well, two of them are. We lost one."

Then he told me his story. He and his family had gone camping with friends in Arizona. They were from Connecticut, and it was the only vacation they ever took. A few days in, their teenage daughter took the car into town. She never returned. A frantic search revealed nothing.

Fearing the worst (kidnapping or enslavement), the man quit his

151

job and became a truck driver. He spent the rest of his career driving throughout the country in search of his daughter.

After being kidnapped at age 11 and enduring 18 years in captivity, Jaycee Dugard sat facing a female police officer. In a separate room, police who had gotten suspicious of the family situation sat questioning her captors.

For a while, Jaycee wouldn't say much. In fact, she even stood up for her kidnappers, who had brainwashed her into thinking that her life in captivity was normal—that the new name they'd given her was her true identity.

Finally, the police officer asked Jaycee what her real name was. Jaycee froze. Afraid to even utter it, she wrote it down on a piece of paper: Jaycee Dugard.

"It was like breaking an evil spell," she said later. "I looked at her and said 'I can see my mom?' She said 'Yes!' "

The bond between those who love each other was never meant to be broken, not through slave auctions, not through abductions, not through divorce, not through death. None of them are natural—none are from God.

Our Separation

The separation between humans and God began with two people huddled in the Garden of Eden, naked and ashamed: "Then the man and his wife heard the sound of the Lord God as he was walking in the garden in the cool of the day, and they hid from the Lord God among the trees of the garden. But the Lord God called to the man, 'Where are you?'" (Gen. 3:8, 9).

Through the years the gulf would continue to widen, even among the people that God chose to bless the world. After leading the Israelites through the Red Sea in a supreme act of grace, the Lord set up a tabernacle in the desert to illustrate just how far humanity had wandered from Him— in case anyone ever felt inclined to think the separation was normal. With its many levels of access—the courtyard, the holy place, the Most Holy Place, the outside of the ark, the inside of the ark, the Shekinah glory—the tabernacle kept all but one person a year out of the immediate presence of God. But, the people were assured, this distance was only temporary. For those who entered God's salvation rest, symbolized by a weekly Sabbath rest, they would commune with Him once more.

But the people would not rest. Of the original 12 tribes of Israel that entered the Promised Land, only a few remained faithful, the most prominent being Judah. Most of them found themselves scattered throughout the world—the so-called lost tribes of Israel. And even the people of Judah, now called Jews, began to exchange worshipping God for worshipping the work of their own hands. One of the things the Jewish people were supposed to do was to let their land rest every seventh year. But the Jews hadn't allowed the land such rest for 490 years, meaning that the land was owed 70 years of rest. So God Himself gave the land its sabbath rest—by delivering the Jewish people to Babylon.

If there was any place on earth the Jews didn't want to go, it was Babylon. No place made them more sick to their stomachs. Babylon, Babylonia— Babel!—was where God had summoned the Hebrews *out* of. Babel was the land of human effort, of worshipping the work of your hands. God had called Abraham *out of* Babel to a land of rest. Now they were right back where they had started. Square one.

But streams of light would pierce the darkness of Babylon. God set an upright Jewish man named Daniel over a group of indigenous wise men called magi. Daniel received messages from the Lord through the angel Gabriel. In one of them he learned that there would be a new period of 490 years—literally "seven seventies"—during which Israel would get another shot to get things right. Seven seventies were "decreed for your people and your holy city to finish transgression, to put an end to sin, to atone for wickedness, to bring in everlasting righteousness, to seal up vision and prophecy and to anoint the most holy" (Dan. 9:24).

Near the end of this period, the angel explained to Daniel, an Anointed One would come. The Hebrew word for "anointed" is "messiah."

Following their 70-year captivity, most of the Jews decided to stay and hang out in the world—now the Persian Empire—rather than return home to Jerusalem. Even those that did go home and settle had mixed feelings. They were excited to be rebuilding their Temple, but as the foundation was laid, those who remembered Solomon's magnificent structure realized that this second Temple wasn't going to be anywhere as nice—and they "wept aloud" (Ezra 3:4).

The people received some unexpected encouragement from two men standing among them: an old prophet named Haggai and a younger one, Zechariah. Haggai reminded everyone that the true glory of Solomon's Temple didn't come from what that king or any other human being brought to it. It wasn't Solomon's Temple but God's. Haggai said: "This is what the

Lord Almighty says: 'In a little while I will once more shake the heavens and the earth, the sea and the dry land. I will shake all nations, and the desired of all nations will come, and I will fill this house with glory,' says the Lord Almighty. 'The silver is mine and the gold is mine,' declares the Lord Almighty. 'The glory of this present house will be greater than the glory of the former house,' says the Lord Almighty" (Haggai 2:6-9).

The glory of this second Temple would be even greater than the first? Things got even more hopeful when Zechariah spoke: "Rejoice greatly, O Daughter of Zion! Shout, Daughter of Jerusalem! See, your king comes to you, righteous and having salvation, gentle and riding on a donkey, on a colt, the foal of a donkey" (Zech. 9:9).

Such prophecies brought great hope to a people struggling just to hang on. The Jewish people at the time had two leaders: a priest named Joshua from the line of Levi and a king-like ruler, Zerubbabel, from the royal line of David. Both the priest and the king were important to the Jews. They believed that there would be not one but two messiahs who would save Israel: a priestly messiah from the tribe of Levi and a kingly one from the tribe of Judah. They did not comprehend the possibility that one person could be both a king and a priest at the same time.

That's why it was startling when the young prophet Zechariah said: "Listen, High Priest Joshua, you and your associates seated before you, who are men symbolic of things to come: I am going to bring my servant, the Branch (Zech. 3:8). "Take the silver and gold and make a crown, and set it on the head of the high priest, Joshua son of Jozadak. Tell him this is what the Lord Almighty says: 'Here is the man whose name is the Branch, and he will branch out from his place and build the temple of the Lord. It is he who will build the temple of the Lord, and he will be clothed with majesty and will sit and rule on his throne. And he will be a priest on his throne'" (Zech. 6:11-13).

"A priest on his throne"? How was that possible? A man named Joshua who's the Branch—the Messiah? Who's both priest and king? What was going on here?

The name Joshua, also appearing as Jeshua, actually wasn't pronounced with a "J" sound. In early English, "J" had a "Y" sound. So Joshua, or Jeshua, was more correctly pronounced Yeshua. That was the Hebrew name. Yeshua means "salvation."

Zechariah wasn't the only prophet who spoke of the Lord Himself coming to the Temple. Malachi did too—but only after a "messenger" came first to "prepare the way" (Mal. 3:1). This messenger was called the "prophet Elijah" (Mal. 4:5), a prophet in Israel who dressed in camelhair and wore a leather belt around his waist (2 Kings 1:8).

After rebuilding the Temple, the Jews resumed regular sacrifices. Shepherds working in some fields about six miles south of Jerusalem, near the small village of Bethlehem, tended the lambs used for Temple sacrifices. Bethlehem was where King David himself had once been a shepherd boy. There was actually a curious little prophecy about the place that had come from the mouth of the prophet Micah: "'But you, Bethlehem Ephrathah, though you are small among the clans of Judah, out of you will come for me one who will be ruler over Israel, whose origins are from of old, from ancient times'. . . . He will stand and shepherd his flock in the strength of the Lord, in the majesty of the name of the Lord his God. And they will live securely, for then his greatness will reach to the ends of the earth. And he will be our peace" (Micah 5:2-5).

With the deaths of the minor prophets, Micah through Malachi, prophecy ceased, and God appeared to go silent for 400 years. That seemed strange, because the Jews were approaching closer and closer to that 490-year (seven seventies) mark prophesied by Daniel. But rather than things getting better, they grew worse and worse. The Jews went from being ruled over by the relatively moderate power of Persia to being controlled by Greece and their young king Alexander the Great. Following Alexander's death, later Greek rulers began persecuting the devout Jews. The height of the persecution saw a pig sacrificed in the Temple. In response, some heroic Jewish fighters, called the Maccabeans, retook Jerusalem and rededicated the Temple. The celebration of this event became a new Jewish holiday called Hanukkah, or the Feast of Lights.

In time, the empire of Rome conquered Judah. They ruled with an iron fist and heavily taxed the Jewish people. The Jews were now spread out, living not just in the south near Jerusalem but all across Palestine. So it became a hassle when the Roman ruler Caesar Augustus ordered that everybody must return to the hometown of their original tribe so they could be counted and taxed. Among the people who began to make travel arrangements was a young engaged couple living up north in a small village near the Sea of Galilee. Named Yosef and Mary, they were descendants of the tribe of Judah, so they would need to journey 80 miles south to Judah to register.

Prior to their departure, Joseph and Mary suddenly received news that would forever change not only their world, but also the entire world. Out of nowhere the same angel Gabriel, who had once visited Daniel, suddenly appeared to Mary and said: "Do not be afraid, Mary, you have found favor with God. You will be with child and give birth to a son, and you are to give him the name Jesus [Yeshua]. He will be great and will be called the Son of the Most High. The Lord God will give him the throne of his father David, and he will reign over the house of Jacob forever; his kingdom will never end" (Luke 1:30-33).

Meanwhile, back in Persia, some men had been studying. They found themselves fascinated with the prophesied coming of the Jewish messiah. Combining their study of the Hebrew Scriptures with their interest in astrology, the Magi set their eyes to the western night sky and began to plan a trip to Judea with their typical cavalry escort and some carefully selected gifts.

Meanwhile, in the late fall, probably October, shepherds in the fields outside Bethlehem were doing what they always did: tending the sheep that would serve as sacrifices in Jerusalem. The flocks were out in the hills because it wasn't the rainy season yet. When the rainy season came, the lambs would be born in the caves around Bethlehem.

But on this fall evening, as the shepherds sat watching their sheep, their world was also suddenly altered—by a sky full of angels. One of the angels said: "Do not be afraid. I bring you good news of great joy that will be for all the people. Today in the town of David a Savior has been born to you; he is Christ the Lord. This will be a sign to you: You will find a baby wrapped in cloths and lying in a manger" (Luke 2:10-12).

After all this time—after so many years of separation—everything was suddenly changing. All types of people, poor and rich, Jews and Gentiles, were being drawn to a humble cave where a newborn named Yeshua lay his soft head. This same Yeshua had once roamed a garden paradise filled with animals, calling out to a young man and woman, "Where are you?" Now he had come back, this time to a dark cave filled with animals, to be together again with a young man and woman. He would bridge the separation, reunite with the human race, put an end to sin, atone for wickedness, bring in everlasting righteousness, and make all things new. Lamb, Priest, King, Yeshua, Messiah, Immanuel. Once more God was with us.

The people who looked for the first coming of Jesus were a blessed and broken group of Sabbathkeepers living in anticipation of the Advent. They were far from perfect; their commitment never came close to their calling.

But God had entrusted them with the treasures of Scripture, both new and old, that reveal to all people their deepest longing: a Savior.

As their blessed and broken counterparts, we long for the return of this same Savior.